Understanding

The Great Gatsby

UNDERSTANDING GREAT LITERATURE

Michael J. Wyly

Lucent Books
10911 Technology Place
San Diego, CA 92127

New and future titles in the Understanding Great Literature
series include:

Understanding *The Catcher in the Rye*
Understanding *Flowers for Algernon*
Understanding *Hamlet*
Understanding *I Am the Cheese*
Understanding *Johnny Tremain*
Understanding *Macbeth*
Understanding *Of Mice and Men*
Understanding *The Outsiders*
Understanding *Romeo and Juliet*
Understanding *The Yearling*

Library of Congress Cataloging-in-Publication Data

Wyly, Michael J., 1970–
  Understanding The Great Gatsby / by Michael J. Wyly.
    p. cm. — (Understanding great literature)
  Includes bibliographical references and index.
  Summary: Discusses the life of F. Scott Fitzgerald and the historical
context, plot, themes, and character analysis of *The Great Gatsby.*
  ISBN 1-56006-997-X (alk. paper)
  1. Fitzgerald, F. Scott (Francis Scott), 1896–1940. Great
Gatsby—Juvenile literature. [1. Fitzgerald, F. Scott (Francis
Scott), 1896–1940. Great Gatsby.] I. Title. II. Series.
  PS3511.I9 G898 2002
  813'—dc21

2001003470

Copyright 2002 by Lucent Books, Inc.
10911 Technology Place, San Diego, California 92127

Printed in the U.S.A.

Contents

FOREWORD

"Except for a living man, there is nothing more wonderful than a book!" wrote the widely respected nineteenth-century teacher and writer Charles Kingsley. A book, he continued, "is a message to us from human souls we never saw. And yet these [books] arouse us, terrify us, teach us, comfort us, open our hearts to us as brothers." There are many different kinds of books, of course; and Kingsley was referring mainly to those containing literature—novels, plays, short stories, poems, and so on. In particular, he had in mind those works of literature that were and remain widely popular with readers of all ages and from many walks of life.

Such popularity might be based on one or several factors. On the one hand, a book might be read and studied by people in generation after generation because it is a literary classic, with characters and themes of universal relevance and appeal. Homer's epic poems, the *Iliad* and the *Odyssey*, Chaucer's *Canterbury Tales*, Shakespeare's *Hamlet* and *Romeo and Juliet*, and Dickens's *A Christmas Carol* fall into this category. Some popular books, on the other hand, are more controversial. Mark Twain's *Huckleberry Finn* and J. D. Salinger's *The Catcher in the Rye*, for instance, have their legions of devoted fans who see them as great literature; while others view them as less than worthy because of their racial depictions, profanity, or other factors.

Still another category of popular literature includes realistic modern fiction, including novels such as Robert Cormier's *I Am the Cheese* and S. E. Hinton's *The Outsiders*. Their keen social insights and sharp character portrayals have consistently reached out to and captured the imaginations of many teenagers and young adults; and for this reason they are often assigned and studied in schools.

These and other similar works have become the "old standards" of the literary scene. They are the ones that people most often read, discuss, and study; and each has, by virtue of its content, critical success, or just plain longevity, earned the right to be the subject of a book examining its content. (Some, of course, like the *Iliad* and *Hamlet*, have been the subjects of numerous books already; but their literary stature is so lofty that there can never be too many books about them!) For millions of readers and students in one generation after another, each of these works becomes, in a sense, an adventure in appreciation, enjoyment, and learning.

The main purpose of Lucent's Understanding Great Literature series is to aid the reader in that ongoing literary adventure. Each volume in the series focuses on a single literary work that a majority of critics and teachers view as a classic and/or that is widely studied and discussed in schools. A typical volume first tells why the work in question is important. Then follow detailed overviews of the author's life, the work's historical background, its plot, its characters, and its themes. Numerous quotes from the work, as well as by critics and other experts, are interspersed throughout and carefully documented with footnotes for those who wish to pursue further research. Also included is a list of ideas for essays and other student projects relating to the work, an appendix of literary criticisms and analyses by noted scholars, and a comprehensive annotated bibliography.

The great nineteenth-century American poet Henry David Thoreau once quipped: "Read the best books first, or you may not have a chance to read them at all." For those who are reading or about to read the "best books" in the literary canon, the comprehensive, thorough, and thoughtful volumes of the Understanding Great Literature series are indispensable guides and sources of enrichment.

INTRODUCTION

The Humanity of *The Great Gatsby*

F. Scott Fitzgerald was one of the first great American writers to have isolated and confronted the question of class in his fiction. Indeed, all of his characters can be considered representatives of the class system of the United States during the early part of the twentieth century. This is especially true of his most influential novel, *The Great Gatsby*, set in the early 1920s. Fitzgerald's ability to incorporate his observations into his novel allows his readers to become aware of the manners and mannerisms of the wealthy American elite of the 1920s as well as the illusions and unanswered dreams that plagued those who desired these riches. *The Great Gatsby* is therefore not only a powerful story, but it also presents a look at American culture in the 1920s.

The Great Gatsby begins with the arrival of the novel's narrator, Nick Carraway, to Long Island Sound. Carraway meets Jay Gatsby while at one of Gatsby's outrageous weekend parties. Afterward, Gatsby asks if Carraway will arrange a secret meeting between him and the married Daisy Buchanan, who is Carraway's cousin. Because of the efforts of Carraway, an affair between Daisy and Gatsby commences, which causes a rivalry between Gatsby and Daisy's husband, the rich elitist Tom Buchanan. This conflict stems from the manner in which the two men gained their wealth:

Whereas Gatsby was engaged in a number of illegal activities, including bootlegging and selling stolen bonds, Tom inherited his wealth and position. Despite his criminal background, however, Gatsby remains the more romantic of the two. He believes in the attainment of ideals, such as his love for Daisy, while Tom is a more calculating and cruel man. Their conflict is soon marred by the death of Tom's secret lover, Myrtle Wilson, whom Daisy accidently runs down while driving Gatsby's car. Myrtle's death provokes her husband to kill the owner of the car. Gatsby is therefore gunned down by the suicidal George Wilson, leaving Carraway to pick up the pieces by arranging Gatsby's funeral while reflecting on the meaning of the story he has just narrated.

The characters of *The Great Gatsby* would seem to have unending possibilities because of their great wealth; yet this access to vast sums of money also means that Fitzgerald's characters are subject to the illusion that money can purchase happiness. Similarly, Fitzgerald milled with the wealthy elite of the United States. Although Fitzgerald did value the prospect of great wealth, he—at least in his fiction—was not taken in by it. As critic Marius Bewley comments,

> [Fitzgerald] instinctively realized the part that money played in creating and supporting a way of life focused on the Ivy League universities, country clubs, trips to the Riviera, and the homes of the wealthy. He is the first American writer who seems to have discovered that such a thing as American class *really* existed. . . . Fitzgerald was enabled to make this discovery because he was almost preternaturally [extraordinarily] aware of the reality that gold lent to the play of appearances that he loved so much. Because he immersed himself so completely in this play of appearances—in swank parties, jazz tunes, alcohol and colored lights—many have questioned the fineness and the discrimination of his intelligence. But what he immersed himself in *was*

7

the America of his time (and almost as much, perhaps, of ours). . . . As an artist, Scott Fitzgerald knew the worst there was to know about all these things, and he knew it with an inwardness and a profoundness. [1]

Consequently, Fitzgerald was able to create such startling characters as the protagonist of *The Great Gatsby*, Jay Gatsby, who rises to riches in the pursuit of an unobtainable ideal, and Tom and Daisy Buchanan, who struggle with their own self-imposed elitism as they shatter the lives of those around them who are less fortunate. And all of these characters are struck with the truth of the nature of wealth: The reality of the human condition is that we strive for ideals and emotions that surpass the influence of money even for the most wealthy of elites.

One only has to listen to the words of the narrator of *The Great Gatsby*, Nick Carraway, to understand the profound depth to which Fitzgerald understood the illusionary power of money and, indeed, the dreams of life itself. In the final lines of the novel, Carraway reflects on the nature of Jay Gatsby:

> He had come a long way to this blue lawn, and his dream must have seemed so close that he could hardly fail to grasp it. He did not know that it was already behind him, some-where back in that vast obscurity beyond the city, where the dark fields of the republic rolled on under the night.

> Gatsby believed in the green light, the orgiastic [frenzied] future that year by year recedes before us. It eluded us then, but that's no matter—tomorrow we will run faster, stretch out our arms farther. . . . And one fine morning—

> So we beat on, boats against the current, borne ceaseless-ly back into the past. [2]

Fitzgerald's novel not only provides its readers with an insight into the characters of *The Great Gatsby*, but it also explores what it is to be a living, dreaming human.

CHAPTER ONE

The Life of F. Scott Fitzgerald

N ear the end of his life, F. Scott Fitzgerald wrote to his only daughter,

If you have anything to say, anything you feel nobody has ever said before, you have got to feel it so desperately that you will find some way to say it that nobody has ever found before, so that the thing you have to say and the way of saying it blend as one matter—as indissolubly as if they were conceived together.[3]

This advice could also be used to describe Fitzgerald's own motivations during his life. For the majority of his life, Fitzgerald sought to establish himself as a writer of unique voice, subject material, and ability with varying degrees of success. Troubled by a

F. Scott Fitzgerald sometimes incorporated the failures of his own life into his novels.

number of failures, even after the publishing of *The Great Gatsby*, as well as the effects of a lifelong drinking problem, F. Scott Fitzgerald continually fought to make a living as a writer. Yet it was these experiences that allowed him to be the writer that he was: His novels are at times intensely autobiographical because he incorporated even the darkest moments of his life into his fiction in order to bring his imagination to life.

The Fitzgeralds

Francis Scott Key Fitzgerald, like the main character of *The Great Gatsby*, was raised primarily in the Midwest. He was born on September 24, 1896, in Saint Paul, Minnesota, to Edward and Mary "Mollie" McQuillan Fitzgerald. While Mollie was pregnant with Scott, her daughters, ages one and three, both died. A few years later Scott's mother had yet another daughter, who died within her first hour, and it would not be until July 1901, with the birth of Scott's sister Annabel, that Scott would not be an only child. Consequently, Mollie coddled and spoiled Scott, the effect of which produced an uneasy relationship between him and his parents.

Mollie was of Irish background, her grandparents having immigrated to the United States to escape poverty. Mollie's family managed to establish a modest fortune, which helped to provide for the Fitzgeralds when Mollie's father died in 1877. She inherited a million-dollar grocery business and $250,000. Indeed, it was Mollie's inheritance that allowed Scott to attend private boarding schools and later Princeton University. Yet this background of financial security and the ability to support her small family was not something that she shared with her husband.

Throughout Scott's young life, Edward Fitzgerald tried to support his family. However, his continual loss of jobs eventually broke his spirit. When Scott was born, Edward managed a wicker furniture company, the American Rattan and Willow Works. In 1898, the business failed. Having no other prospects in Saint Paul, he moved his family to Buffalo, New York, where he secured a position as a soap salesman with Proctor and Gamble. For the next ten years, in the employment of Proctor and Gamble, Edward moved his family between Buffalo and Syracuse.

However, by 1908 Edward was again out of work. He decided to move back to Saint Paul, where he took a lowly job with a family friend's real estate office. But the damage to Edward's pride had been done. As Scott described later in life, "That morning he had gone out a comparatively young man, a man full of strength, full of confidence. He came home that evening an old man, a completely old man. He had lost his essential drive, his immaculateness of purpose. He was a failure the rest of his days."[4] Unable to support his family, Edward and his family had to rely on the dwindling fortune of his wife for the rest of their lives. Edward also began to drink—a condition that would later develop into a severe drinking problem.

Yet it was not his father's drinking but the overprotective attitude of his mother that hindered Scott's relationship with his parents. Mollie constantly worried about his health (she bundled Scott into so much protective clothing that he would develop a hatred for restrictive clothing for the rest of his life). She urged Scott to show off in public and gave into all of his childish whims. She did not teach him self-discipline nor strong study habits, and Scott himself would later chastise her for this.

Even more importantly, she did not encourage Scott to become a writer; instead, she expected him to have a career in either business or the military. She even went so far as to throw away Scott's earliest literary efforts. As Scott later reported in one of his letters, "My mother did me the disservice of throwing away all but two of my very young efforts [at writing]—way back at twelve and thirteen, and later I found that the surviving fragments had more quality than some of the stuff written in the tightened-up days of seven or eight years later."[5] To the contrary, Scott's father, despite his personal problems, was the primary influence on Scott's career goals. Edward introduced Scott to poetry and literature. And when his son expressed the desire to write, he encouraged him to pursue his literary aspirations.

An Early Writer

With his father's encouragement, Scott began to write seriously when he was only twelve years old and attending the Saint Paul Academy. Yet despite his literary ambitions, the protective habits of his mother would also have their effect, for he tended to ignore his studies in favor of writing. This habit would haunt him throughout his scholastic life.

At the Saint Paul Academy, Scott wrote plays for the Elizabethan drama club, a student-run dramatic group that performed for charity during the summer. Scott also published his first story in 1909 in *Now and Then*, the school magazine. Because all of his energies went to these projects, his grades suffered. Both of his parents were disappointed in his academic performance, and Scott was sent to a Catholic boarding school, the Newman Academy in Hackensack, New Jersey. They hoped that a more strict learning environment would push Scott to academic excellence. However, this was not the case, partly due to early experimentation with alcohol. As biographer Matthew J. Bruccoli summarizes,

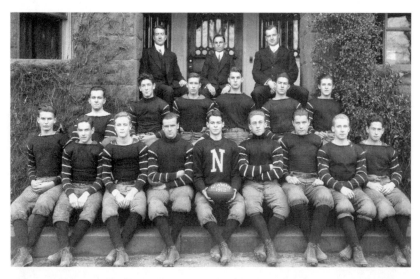

At the Newman Academy, Fitzgerald (front row, third from left) played football but failed to achieve academic excellence.

Scott and his friends had experimented with drugstore sherry in Saint Paul. In 1913 he began to try stronger liquors at Newman. He had his first whiskey in March, an April *Ledger* entry notes that he was "Tight [drunk] at Susquehanna." His academic situation remained shaky; his Newman school record shows that he failed four courses in two years. . . . It is normal—almost obligatory—for literary geniuses to get poor grades in math and science: but Scott did not distinguish himself in English courses, either.[6]

Although Scott's academic records were less than exceptional, he did make two very important discoveries that would profoundly affect his future writing career.

The first discovery was the acquaintance of Father Sigourney Webster Fay, who often invited Scott to his home to encourage his aspirations to become a writer. In fact, Father Fay would be the one who later encouraged Fitzgerald to write his first novel, *This Side of Paradise.* Fay also introduced Scott to the well-connected Shane Leslie, who would recommend the novel to Scribner's publishing company. Scott would develop a lifetime relationship with Scribner's that included the publishing of *The Great Gatsby.* In many ways, Father Fay became Scott's surrogate father. Scott even provided a portrait of Fay in *This Side of Paradise:*

> He was intensely ritualistic, startlingly dramatic, loved the idea of God enough to be celibate, and rather liked his neighbor.
>
> Children adored him because he was like a child; youth reveled in his company because he was still a youth, and couldn't be shocked. In the proper land and century he might have been a Richelieu [a nineteenth century French cardinal noted for his belief in the importance of secular affairs] at present he was a very moral, very religious (if not particularly pious) clergyman, making a great mystery about pulling rusty wires, and appreciating life to the fullest, if not entirely enjoying it.[7]

Scott's second discovery involved the nature of the Newman Academy. Newman was typically reserved for children of well-to-do parents who sought entrance to Princeton, Harvard, and other elite universities. While at Newman, Scott became profoundly aware of his status as a "poor boy" at a rich-person's school. His efforts at making friends were, for the most part, snubbed, and he was teased for his lack of money. Later in life, Fitzgerald reflected on this aspect of his childhood:

> I was unhappy because I was cast in a situation where everybody thought I ought to behave just as they behaved—and I didn't have the courage to shut up and go my own way, anyhow.

> For example, there was a rather dull boy at school named Percy, whose approval, I felt, for some unfathomable reason, I must have. So, for the sake of this negligible cipher, I started out to let out as much of my mind as I had under mild cultivation.[8]

But neither of these discoveries contributed to an increased perseverance in his studies. Despite his lackluster success at Newman, Scott Fitzgerald decided to attend Princeton University in 1913. Not surprisingly, his poor performance at Newman meant that he needed to pass an entrance exam, which he failed. What is surprising, however, is that Fitzgerald managed to secure an interview with the admissions officer and thereby talked his way into a probationary acceptance. He would be allowed to attend Princeton, but he would still need to prove himself academically to avoid expulsion.

The Princeton Years: 1913–1917

Although Fitzgerald found himself relatively in the same position at Princeton University as at Newman—he was still the poor student in an institution reserved for the elite—he learned the social games that gained him acceptance from his peers. These lessons were in part due to his growing success as a writer. In his first year,

Fitzgerald was invited to join the prestigious Triangle Club, a student-run group that produced and performed musical comedies. In fact, Fitzgerald's first written entry, "Fie! Fie! Fi-Fi!," won the competition for the next play to be produced. With this achievement, Fitzgerald began to establish his reputation as a writer at Princeton. He also became a member of the editorial board of the *Princetonian* and contributed to the university publications the *Tiger* and *Nassau Lit.* He was consequently invited to join one of the most elite campus clubs, the Cottage Club. Biographer Arthur Mizener describes the importance of campus clubs to Princeton life:

At Princeton, Fitzgerald gained social skills that helped him interact with his elite peers.

A Princeton club, apart from providing a place to eat, play billiards, and to take a girl on week-ends . . . does not even pretend to offer anything. The function of the Princeton clubs is to provide a system of grading people according to social distinction at the middle of the sophomore year. Once that is done, their serious purpose has been fulfilled.[9]

These experiences allowed Fitzgerald to enter the social mainstream that had been denied him while at Newman. He began to meet elite people, including his first love, sixteen-year-old Ginevra King. King was beautiful, rich, and socially secure. And Fitzgerald intensely pursued her despite the fact that she lived in Chicago. From 1915 until 1917, Fitzgerald and King corresponded via letters, all of which spoke of their love for each other with typical adolescent fervor. In one such letter, Fitzgerald writes to King,

"Oh, it's so hard to write you what I really feel when I think about you so much; you've gotten to mean to me a dream that I can't put on paper any more." [10]

However, for all of Fitzgerald's efforts at being accepted amongst the elitist classes, Ginevra King broke off the affair primarily due to Fitzgerald's less-distinguished background. The effect that this had on Fitzgerald can be glimpsed in the fact that he had all of King's letters bound into a 227-page typed book, which he kept with him for many years to come, even though King destroyed all traces of his correspondence with her. Indeed, King became a model for many of Scott's future characters, including the heroine of *This Side of Paradise.*

Yet the loss of Ginevra was not Fitzgerald's only disappointment during this time. Despite his extraordinary efforts at gaining acceptance to Princeton, Fitzgerald continued to ignore his studies, the effects of which inhibited even his literary ambitions. Although the comedy "Fie! Fie! Fi-Fi!" was accepted, for example, Fitzgerald was denied the opportunity to tour with the Triangle Club because he was on academic probation. By the end of his sophomore year, he was almost expelled on academic grounds. He argued that he should be allowed special treatment because he was an artist. To make matters worse, Fitzgerald contracted malaria in November 1915. His admittance to the infirmary, in combination with his low grades, meant that he had to temporarily withdraw from the university. As a result, he had to repeat his junior year in 1916–1917. After that, Fitzgerald decided to join the army. He never did obtain a degree, from Princeton or any other university.

Military Service

The year 1917 brought about the involvement of the United States in the Great War in Europe (World War I). Disheartened with Princeton as well as his unsuccessful romance with Ginevra King, Fitzgerald gave in to his mother's initial wish that he become a soldier. In July 1917 he took the examinations to enter the army as an officer. In October, Second Lieutenant Scott Fitzgerald was sent to

Fort Leavenworth, Kansas, for training. However, like his academic career, Fitzgerald's military career was less than exemplary.

News of soldiers dying in Europe was an everyday event. Fitzgerald therefore resigned himself to the idea that he would probably die once his company was shipped overseas. Indeed, it was because he expected that he would be killed that he wrote with such a furious passion while at the officer training camps. Even if he did survive the war, Fitzgerald did not think he would be able to write in the same way. As he once wrote in the margins of a manuscript, "I've got to write now, for when the war's over I won't be able to see these things as important—even now they are fading out against the background of the map of Europe. I'll never be able to do it again; well done or poorly. So I'm writing almost desperately—and so futily." [11]

This sense of desperate urgency led Fitzgerald to write during his training classes. As he describes,

Every evening, concealing my pad behind Small Problems for Infantry, I write paragraph after paragraph on a somewhat edited history of me and my imagination. The outline of twenty-two chapters, four of them in verse, was made, two chapters were completed; and then I was detected and the game was up. [12]

Fitzgerald was convinced that he would not survive the combat in Europe during World War I.

After he was caught, and under threat of disciplinary action, Fitzgerald began writing on weekends in the officers' club. In this way, he completed a 120,000-word novel in three months. The novel was titled *The Romantic Egoist*, after heavy revisions and a new title, *This Side of Paradise*, this piece would later be his first published novel.

Despite the discipline Fitzgerald developed as a writer, he continued to be a horrible soldier and officer. He regularly misled his platoon due to his ineptitude, and during combat exercises Fitzgerald mistakenly commanded his men to fire on another platoon on his own side. Indeed, it was lucky for him that the war ended on November 11, 1918, just as he was about to be sent to France.

Love and the First Novel

Two events occurred while Fitzgerald was in the army, both of which dramatically affected his life and writing career. In 1918, while stationed at Camp Sheridan near Montgomery, Alabama, Fitzgerald received a letter announcing the marriage of Ginevra King (an event he uses in *The Great Gatsby* to explain Gatsby's own obsession with Daisy Fay). A short time later he met the second love of his life, the eighteen-year-old Zelda Sayre, the woman who would one day become his wife and who encouraged him to complete and publish his first novel.

Unlike his premilitary love of King, Sayre was not wealthy; however, she did come from a prominent Alabama family in which her father was an associate justice of the Alabama Supreme Court. Sayre was known throughout Montgomery as a beautiful but outlandish girl with a quick, and often dark, wit. She was also known for her sexual promiscuity, although some biographers suggest that she was probably more of a tease who enjoyed the scandalous reputation. Virginia Foster Durr, who was an acquaintance of Sayre's in Montgomery, describes her as follows:

> Zelda was like a vision of beauty dancing by. She was funny, amusing, the most popular girl, envied by all of

the others, worshipped and adored, besieged by all the boys. She *did* try to shock. At a dance she pinned mistletoe on the back of her skirt, as if to challenge the young men to kiss her bottom. . . . She was always like a visiting film star: radiant, glowing, desired by all.[13]

Taken in by the beauty and charm of Sayre, Fitzgerald resolved that upon his discharge from the army, he would win her for himself despite her numerous admirers. Fitzgerald told Sayre that she reminded him of the heroine of his novel and sent her a chapter to prove the resemblance. Ultimately impressed with Fitzgerald, Sayre agreed to marry him, and they were secretly engaged. Despite Fitzgerald's protests, Sayre refused to marry until he could prove a steady income. Fitzgerald would either have to make money through his writing or lose Sayre.

Fitzgerald moved to New York City, where he obtained a job writing advertising slogans. During the evenings, he wrote numerous stories that he sent to the literary magazines; yet each was rejected. Fitzgerald later reflected on the frustrations of his initial stint in New York:

As I hovered ghost-like in the Plaza Red Room of a Saturday afternoon, or went to lush and liquid garden parties in the East Sixties or tippled with Princetonians in the Biltmore Bar I was haunted always by my other life—my drab room in the Bronx, my square foot of the subway, my fixation on the day's letter from Alabama—would it come and what would it say?—my shabby suits, my poverty, and love. . . . I was a failure—mediocre at advertising and unable to get started as a writer.[14]

In 1919 Fitzgerald made the decision to move back to Saint Paul to rewrite the novel he had begun while in the army. However, on September 16, 1919, eight days before Fitzgerald's twenty-third birthday, Max Perkins of Scribner and Sons accepted the novel. In Perkins's letter to Fitzgerald, he writes, "I am very glad personally to be able to write you that we are all for publishing your book, *This Side of Paradise*. . . . This book is so different that it is hard to prophesy how it will sell but we are all for taking a chance and supporting it with vigor."[15] Through the publication of *This Side of Paradise*, Fitzgerald met the literary agent Harold Ober, who became one of Fitzgerald's closest friends and advisers for most of his life. In fact, Ober would later become responsible for selling many of Fitzgerald's stories to literary magazines. This would provide Fitzgerald with the means to live so he would be able to devote himself solely to writing.

With the announcement of his upcoming novel, Fitzgerald began to experience literary success. From September to December of that same year, he sold nine short stories, mostly to the *Saturday Evening Post*. On the heels of these sales, Fitzgerald returned several times to Montgomery to convince Zelda Sayre that he had proved himself and that they should marry. Eventually, Sayre agreed, and they were finally married on March 26, 1920, in New York at Saint Patrick's Cathedral.

As if to highlight the event, *This Side of Paradise* was released on April 3 of that same year and was an instant success: The first run sold out within twenty-four hours and would go on to sell almost fifty thousand copies by the end of the year. Additionally, Fitzgerald's first collection of short stories, composed of the stories he had sold to magazines, was published later that year under the title *Flappers and Philosophers*. For an excited Fitzgerald, it seemed as if everything were finally coming together.

Newlyweds and Mixed Success

The years following Fitzgerald's marriage to Zelda, however, were a mixture of success and a sense of personal failure. Although Fitzgerald's career as a writer progressed as well as he could hope with respect to continued publications and the earning of money, it was also marked by his growing disappointment in the growth, quality, and consistency of his work.

After the marriage, Zelda became pregnant. She and Fitzgerald traveled to Europe on May 3, 1920. It was the first time that either of them had been abroad. However, because of the pregnancy, the couple returned to Fitzgerald's home in Saint Paul after three months. On October 26, 1920, Zelda gave birth to their only child, a daughter, Frances Scott "Scottie" Fitzgerald. The newlyweds and their newborn daughter lived in Saint Paul briefly and then moved to New York City. While in New York, Fitzgerald finished his second novel, *The Beautiful and Damned,* which was published on March 4, 1922. That September a second collection of his short stories, *Tales of the Jazz Age,* was published.

Despite his literary successes, the fast pace of the New York lifestyle began to take its toll. He and Zelda were increasingly caught up in the social life of 1920s New York. Drinking, dancing, and outings became the norm. As Mizener describes,

Zelda Sayre became Fitzgerald's wife and motivated him to publish his first novel.

[Fitzgerald and Zelda] were both at ease being New Yorkers now, and they were having a wonderful time. Moreover, they wanted to see others have a good time. Between them they could create . . . a charmed and happy world, and they loved doing it. So they played their parts as prince and princess of the confident and eager kingdom of youth with what one of their friends called "an almost theatrical innocence." [16]

This meant that Fitzgerald had substantially less time and energy to devote to his writing. Finally, to escape the elite social scene of New York, the Fitzgeralds moved to Great Neck, located on Long Island Sound just outside of New York City, in October 1922. But instead of leaving the fast-paced scene behind them,

Fitzgerald and Zelda simply transplanted it. The drinking sometimes lasted all weekend. Fitzgerald would occasionally have to spend a night in jail for unruly and drunken behavior. The Fitzgeralds' rented house became a stop-over point for uninvited guests.

Yet Fitzgerald still managed to support his family through the writing of short fiction, something he could accomplish easier although he regarded the longer form of the novel as his truer form of artistic expression. Fitzgerald's agent, Harold Ober, sold eleven stories and seven essays for him between November 1923 and April 1924, earning Fitzgerald the sum of $22,000. Indeed, Fitzgerald was now earning as much as $2,000 per story (as compared to the $150 he earned for his first published story, "The Cut-Glass Bowl"). Not all of his efforts were as well received, however. In November 1923 his play *The Vegetable* opened in Atlantic City, but it was a flop. The play received minimal attendance, horrible reviews, and closed after its opening night. Fitzgerald was severely disappointed at this failure as he had had great faith in the play.

His disappointments were not limited to the failure of the play, though. The constant partying had taken its toll on him, both physically and emotionally. As he reflects in a letter to his editor at Scribner's, Max Perkins,

> It is only in the last four months that I've realized how much I've—well, almost deteriorated in the three years since I finished *The Beautiful and Damned*. The last four months of course I've worked but in the two years—over two years—before that, I produced exactly one play, half a dozen short stories and three or four articles—an average of about one hundred words a day. If I'd spent this time reading or traveling or doing anything—even staying healthy—it'd be different but I spent it uselessly, neither in study nor in contemplation but only in drinking and raising hell generally. [17]

Additionally, Fitzgerald was not satisfied with the quality of his work. His older novels, and notably *The Beautiful and Damned*, were, he felt, an attempt to mimic the other established writers of his era, especially the novelist Theodore Dreiser. He disdained his short fiction, regarding it as too popular and trite. And his new novel, what would eventually become *The Great Gatsby*, was barely under way because his lifestyle prohibited him from working on it.

In May 1924 Fitzgerald wrote Perkins that his next novel would be very different from the previous ones but that he would need to leave the country in order to find the sustained quiet he required to write. With Perkins's aid, the Fitzgeralds left the New York scene. They traveled to Europe and settled on the Mediterranean coast in the south of France. On parting, Fitzgerald vowed that he would not return until he had accomplished something great.

The Great Gatsby and European Life

The Fitzgeralds would spend the next two and a half years in Europe and would travel to Rome, Capri, Antibes, and Paris. But it was during their first year while in Saint Raphael that Fitzgerald accomplished his great novel *The Great Gatsby*. However, its completion contributed to unforeseen difficulties between him and Zelda.

On their arrival in France in May, Fitzgerald stopped drinking to work on his new novel, *Trilmachio*, in which he used many of his New York experiences. He submitted his manuscript to Scribner's after only seven months, but after receiving the proof sheets of the novel, Fitzgerald made heavy revisions, including deleting and adding whole chapters and changing the title to *The Great Gatsby*. Some of these changes were in response to Perkins's

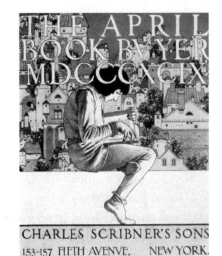

Editors at Scribner's liked the manuscript for The Great Gatsby *but Fitzgerald still made many revisions.*

criticisms, as Fitzgerald explains in one letter to his editor: "I myself didn't know what Gatsby looked like or was engaged in and you felt it. If I'd known it and kept it from you you'd have been too impressed with my knowledge to protest. This is a complicated idea but I'm sure you'll understand. But I know now."[18] Fitzgerald's newest and most famous novel was first published on April 10, 1925. Shortly thereafter Fitzgerald also published his third collection of short stories, *All the Sad Young Men*.

However, Fitzgerald's dedication to his novel was not without its costs. In September 1924, while he wrote, Zelda found herself alone for a considerable amount of time and so continued to go out by herself. In the course of her outings, she met a young French aviation officer, Edouard Josanne. The two began what would be a short-lived affair. Fitzgerald later reported that Zelda had asked him for a divorce so that she could marry her French lover, but that divorce never happened. Instead, Zelda sent Josanne away. Fitzgerald and Zelda tried to mend their relationship, but Fitzgerald would never again feel as close to Zelda as he had before the affair. In fact, he commented later in his life that Zelda's betrayal was something that was never fully repaired.

Fellow author Ernest Hemingway was a good friend of Fitzgerald for years.

Probably the best thing to happen to Fitzgerald while in Europe was his relationship with Ernest Hemingway, a young American author who would go on to win the Nobel Prize in literature. At the advice of friends, Fitzgerald searched out Hemingway while in Paris. The two became friends for many years to come. In fact, Fitzgerald brought Perkins's attention to Hemingway's first novel, *The Sun Also Rises*. Later, after Fitzgerald's death, Hemingway would dedicate a chapter to Fitzgerald in his memoirs, *A Movable Feast*.

To compound Fitzgerald's recent troubles with Zelda, *The Great Gatsby* was not received by the public or the critics with the same enthusiasm as his previous novels. Indeed, although *The Great Gatsby* is now considered his masterpiece, by the end of the year it had sold only twenty thousand copies, barely enough to repay Scribner's for the advances they had already given him. It would not be until 1926, when the author William Brady adapted *The Great Gatsby* to the stage in New York, that Fitzgerald would make money from his novel: He earned six thousand dollars for the sale of the dramatic rights.

Following the stage production, Fitzgerald also received another sixteen thousand dollars for the movie rights from Warner Brothers. This purchase was to begin an on-again, off-again relationship between Fitzgerald and Hollywood. He also signed a contract with *Liberty* magazine for thirty-five thousand dollars for the prepublication rights to his fourth novel, assuming the manuscript was approved by *Liberty* and was delivered by January 1, 1927. However, he did not turn in a manuscript, and it took him nine years to complete it.

Zelda's Breakdowns

In December 1926 the Fitzgeralds returned to the United States, whereupon Fitzgerald was offered a scriptwriting position by United Artists for a silent motion picture starring Considine Talmadge. The contract stipulated that Fitzgerald would be paid twelve thousand dollars for the script. The studio offered to pay him thirty-five hundred dollars of the amount in advance, and he would receive the balance once the film was released. However, Fitzgerald's script, "Lipstick," was not accepted because Talmadge did not approve of it. Upset that he had made less in ten weeks than he would have had he continued writing stories for the *Saturday Evening Post*, Fitzgerald vowed not to work again in Hollywood. Although he would write fifty-five stories for the *Post* from 1927 until 1933, he would also break his last vow and again work with the Hollywood studios.

Anxious to complete his fourth novel, Fitzgerald gave into Zelda's appeals to return to Europe. In 1928 they returned for the summer, and in March 1929 they resided abroad for another two and a half years. These were anxious times for Fitzgerald. He could not seem to put his next novel together and was, therefore, continually reliant on his short-story output. In addition, Zelda's outlandish behavior was becoming more and more uncontrollable. In 1930 she suffered a major emotional breakdown and was sent to a clinic in Switzerland for sixteen months. Most of what Fitzgerald earned from his writing went toward his wife's hospital bills and his incessant partying. To make matters more difficult, Fitzgerald's father died in January 1931, and Zelda's father became seriously ill and later died in November of that same year.

In light of all that occurred, Fitzgerald brought his family back to the United States in September 1931. On their return, Fitzgerald was again offered work in Hollywood, this time by Metro-Goldwyn-Meyer (MGM) Studios. (While Fitzgerald was in Europe, talking pictures had already revolutionized the movie-picture industry. As a result, popular writers were in constant demand to work on the scripts.) Fitzgerald left his wife and child with Zelda's mother in Montgomery to travel to the West Coast.

In Hollywood, Scott was commissioned to collaborate with other staff members on the movie version of Katherine Brush's recent best-selling novel *Red-Headed Woman*. However, Fitzgerald's second experience with Hollywood would leave as bitter of a taste as his first. After an argument with the staff over the quality of the script, he simply walked out on MGM studios in disgust. The staff, as well as MGM's vice president in charge of production, Irving Thalberg, blamed Fitzgerald for having run out on the job and breaching his contract.

In reaction, Fitzgerald returned to the East Coast in 1932 and moved his family outside of Baltimore. That same summer Zelda experienced her second emotional breakdown, and Fitzgerald was again forced to hospitalize her. At the hospital, Zelda was formally diagnosed with the mental disorder schizophrenia. From then on, she would be in and out of mental hospitals for the rest of her life. (She would also write a novel, *Save Me the Waltz*, which would be published with Fitzgerald's assistance but would earn mostly poor reviews and very little money.) And, although Fitzgerald paid for the treatment with the money he made from his writing, they would rarely spend time together after this point, although they would correspond frequently.

Hollywood

During the time of Zelda's second institutionalization, Fitzgerald continued to live his life of excess and heavy drinking. Yet despite his alcoholism and the difficulties imposed by Zelda's condition, he did manage to continue writing. Fitzgerald finally finished the first draft of his fourth novel, *Tender Is the Night* (which he had started in 1925) in September 1933. And between 1934 and 1937, he wrote the Crack-Up stories, an autobiographical collection that provides an especially dark look into the lives of the Fitzgeralds. Despite these successes, Fitzgerald was sinking further and further into debt. In addition, Fitzgerald now had to pay for his daughter's education since she was attending boarding school.

In September 1936 Fitzgerald's mother died, leaving him the money left over from the McQuillan fortune. The money considerably helped him pay his family's bills. However, Fitzgerald was becoming increasingly more desperate because his stories had stopped selling. So when MGM Studios proposed that Fitzgerald work for them again despite their previous disagreements over *Red-Headed Woman*, he accepted their terms: one thousand dollars a week for six months; MGM would renew the contract for another six months if they were pleased with his work and if he remained sober. Fitzgerald remained optimistic and ambitious. As he remarks in a letter to his daughter, Scottie, written while on the train to Hollywood,

> I must be very tactful but keep my hand on the wheel from the start—find out the key man from among the bosses and the most malleable from among the collaborators—then

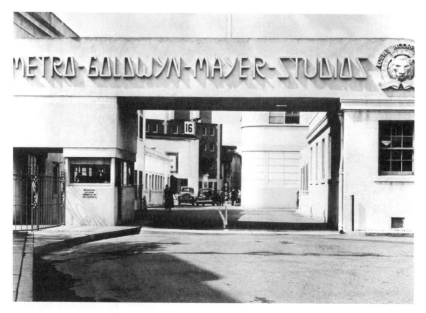

In 1936, MGM Studios producers employed Fitzgerald as a writer, despite the rocky working relationship he had had with them in the past.

fight the rest tooth and nail until, in fact or in effect, I'm alone on the picture. That's the only way I can do my best work. Given a break I can make them double this contract in less than two years. [19]

For a while, Fitzgerald was back on track. He worked with MGM for the next eighteen months. He stayed in contact with Zelda and his daughter by writing letters. And in the summer of 1937, he met the next (and last) great love of his life, Sheilah Graham, with whom he had a long-lasting affair. He also started discussing plans for his next novel, *The Last Tycoon*, a novel based on the life of Thalberg, the MGM vice president. Fitzgerald therefore desired to work for MGM through 1939 so he would be able to put aside the money he would need to buy him the time for his latest novel.

However, Fitzgerald's drinking eventually got the better of him. He began to work with Walter Wanger, who was going to New Hampshire to film *Winter Carnival*. Fitzgerald was ill, but he decided to take the job anyway because he needed the money. While traveling to Dartmouth in a plane, he was offered champagne by an unsuspecting coworker and proceeded to get drunk. He disgraced the whole party when presented to the Dartmouth welcoming committee and was fired by Wanger on the spot. Fitzgerald then went to New York City, where he later turned up at a hospital drunk and ill with pneumonia. The doctors in New York later informed him that he would be dead within the year if he did not stop drinking alcohol.

The Last Days

Fitzgerald's last days were spent sober and living in Encino, California, with Sheilah Graham. He was too ill to take jobs offered during the spring and summer of 1939, but when he was feeling better in September, the job offers disappeared. He was unable to find movie work until February 1940. Indeed, a number of telling letters were written to Scottie in which Fitzgerald described his morose vision of himself—in one, he told her that she need only look at her parents to know what she must not become.

Fitzgerald was bitter not only about the movie industry but the publishing one as well. In 1940 he became angry with Ober, his agent for over twenty years, over a story that Ober had offered for sale that was rejected by the magazines. Ober sent the rejected story back to Fitzgerald with the comments of a well-known editor. Fitzgerald sent a proud, pathetic letter to Ober, which ended the twenty-year relationship. Fitzgerald continued to work in Hollywood, both for Columbia and Twentieth Century Fox studios. And he continued to make progress on *The Last Tycoon*, although slowly; as he describes in a letter to Zelda, "The novel is as hard as pulling teeth but that is because it is in its early character-planting phase. I feel people so less intently than I once did so that this is harder. It means welding together hundreds of stray impressions and incidents to form the fabric of entire personalities." [20]

All work came to a halt for Fitzgerald, however, on November 28, 1940. The victim of a heart attack, he was confined to bed rest. Upset that this would put *The Last Tycoon* behind schedule (he had hoped to finish it by January 1941), Fitzgerald resisted his physician's advice. On December 20, 1940, he completed the first episode of chapter 6 of *The Last Tycoon*. The next day he experienced a second heart attack and died. F. Scott Fitzgerald was forty-four years old. On March 10, 1948, Zelda died in a fire at Highland Sanitarium. A year after Fitzgerald's death, the unfinished novel, *The Last Tycoon*, was published.

Thus, F. Scott Fitzgerald was truly a writer until the bitter end. And despite the mixed success of his work and its acceptance, his dedication to creating literature has left its indelible mark on American fiction. This is especially true of *The Great Gatsby*, the first novel to confront many of the issues surrounding the 1920s, an era with which Fitzgerald was so intimate because of his moneyed friends and lifestyle. Indeed, the biographical nature of *The Great Gatsby*, as well as Fitzgerald's other works, was one of its trademarks and arguably one of the primary reasons for its continuing success so many years later.

CHAPTER TWO

The Jazz Age, Gangsters, and the American Dream

P rior to the publication of *The Great Gatsby*, F. Scott Fitzgerald had anticipated that it would outsell both of his previous novels, *The Other Side of Paradise* and *The Beautiful and Damned*, which had already established his reputation as an author. Although *The Great Gatsby* was eventually regarded as Fitzgerald's masterwork, its reception by the general public was mediocre at best. Very few contemporaries, most of whom were fellow writers, appreciated the new voice and style that Fitzgerald's third and finest novel embodied. Ironically, as the novel itself became accepted, it was Fitzgerald who became the novel's strongest critic. In a letter to his editor, Max Perkins, Fitzgerald regarded the novel's structure and its ability to communicate ideas as imperfect. He concluded that he had simply managed to mask these inadequacies with beautiful prose.

For the modern reader, however, there can be no doubt that *The Great Gatsby* provides a unique insight into the American condition during the 1920s. Indeed, because Fitzgerald was a product of the era, he was able to incorporate his own experiences and publicize contemporary events to create the intricate and rich world of Jay Gatsby. Thus, *The Great Gatsby* is not only a novel but also a lens by which the reader may view American lifestyles during the 1920s Jazz Age.

The Publication and Reception of *The Great Gatsby*

Prior to the publication of *The Great Gatsby*, Fitzgerald was optimistic about its importance. In a letter to one confidante, Edmund Wilson, Fitzgerald writes, "My book is wonderful." Similarly, he writes to John Peale Bishop, "The novel I'm sure of. It's marvelous."[21] Indeed, Fitzgerald felt optimistic about the novel and its financial potential. As biographer Henry Dan Piper explains,

> In January, Fitzgerald had optimistically predicted that the book would sell at least eighty-thousand copies— almost twice that of his other books. He had even volunteered to cut his regular twenty percent royalty back to fifteen as a reward to Scribner's for its continued faith in him! When *College Humor* offered $10,000 for the pre-publication serial rights to *Gatsby*, he turned it down in the hope that they would bring at least $35,000.[22]

To Fitzgerald's dismay, however, a combination of factors inhibited the novel's immediate success. Much of the initial rejection of the novel had to do with its steamy content. Before the novel's release, *Cosmopolitan* and *Liberty* magazines had expressed interest in serializing it; afterward, both magazines decided that the content was too offensive. In a letter to Fitzgerald, the editor of *Liberty* explained that *The Great Gatsby* was "too ripe for us. . . . We could not publish this story with as many mistresses and as much adultery as there is in it."[23]

Even more unexpectedly, many booksellers refused to carry the novel on account of its less-than-expected size. As Piper explains,

> A number of book sellers [canceled] their advanced orders for the novel after discovering that it was to be only 218 pages long. The American reading public, one of them

explained to Perkins, expected a great deal more reading matter than that in a two-dollar novel. After all, the *Saturday Evening Post* contained two-hundred pages every week, and only cost a nickel![24]

To Fitzgerald's further dismay, the international market rejected his book because overseas publishers felt that a non-American audience would not be interested. As the editor of William Collins Sons of London, which had published Fitzgerald's previous novels, wrote at the time, "The British public would not make head or tail of it, and . . . it would not sell. . . . The point is that the atmosphere of the book is extraordinarily foreign to the English reader, and he would simply not believe in it."[25]

Also complicating matters, most of the reviews upon its publication were not favorable. Although the *Dial,* a New York based literary periodical, described *The Great Gatsby* as "one of the finest contemporary novels"[26] and the *Saturday Evening Post* (which had published most of Fitzgerald's short fiction) stated that it had "high occasions of felicitous, almost magic craftsmanship,"[27] most reviewers were not nearly as appreciative. As biographer Kenneth Eble describes, "Indeed, most of the reviews which reached the widest of audiences were mostly unfavorable. . . . The *Herald Tribune* called it 'negligible,' 'uncurbed melodrama,' 'a tragedy with the flavor of skimmed milk.'"[28] Even favorable reviews failed to satisfy Fitzgerald, though. In a letter to Edmund Wilson, Fitzgerald writes, "Of all the reviews, even the most enthusiastic, not one had the slightest idea of what the book was about."[29]

Dorothy Parker was one of several authors who highly praised The Great Gatsby.

However, the exceptions to Fitzgerald's criticisms were noteworthy. Although the quality of Fitzgerald's newest novel may have eluded the majority of the public, its virtues did not escape other authors of the era. The poet T. S. Eliot and the novelists Willa Cather and Dorothy Parker sent letters of praise. The young Ernest Hemingway spoke well of it to his friends and later reiterated these comments to Fitzgerald. And the novelist Edith Wharton invited Fitzgerald to join her for tea—an invite that Fitzgerald accepted.

The novel, as a result, only sold twenty thousand copies in its first year. But in time, Fitzgerald's masterwork did become more universally appreciated. A year after its publication it was published in England by Chatto and Windus. And in 1934 its inclusion in the Modern Library series established *The Great Gatsby* as a recognized contemporary masterpiece, primarily because of its insights into the 1920s.

The Jazz Age

Much of the reason for *The Great Gatsby*'s successful depiction of 1920s America was because Fitzgerald lived the experiences about which he wrote. The armistice of November 1918, which signified the end of World War I, gave way to the era known as the Roaring Twenties or, to use Fitzgerald's coinage, the Jazz Age. Characterized by an increase in money never before seen, many newly self-made millionaires made their presence known, especially in New York. They mingled with those people whose families had possessed quantities of money for generations. Indeed, Fitzgerald's Jazz Age was not really about jazz as a musical medium; instead, the term meant a spontaneity of action characteristic of the young, well-off partygoers with whom he associated.

Much of Fitzgerald's historical accuracy came from his own experiences in Great Neck, his model for the areas of East and West Egg in the novel. Although Fitzgerald did not have anywhere near the amount of money of the fictional Gatsby, he certainly ran a Gatsby-like household. As Piper explains, "Many New York friends had gotten in the habit of treating the Fitzgerald residence as a roadhouse. . . . 'Weekend parties' there had a way of stretching from one weekend to the next."[30] These parties and

The parties of the Roaring Twenties were an inspiration for The Great Gatsby.

others that Fitzgerald attended consisted of numerous celebrities and other well-known people. As Piper describes:

> The Great Neck section had attracted [Fitzgerald and his wife] because of its convenient commuting distance to the city; also, it had recently become popular with a great many actors, directors, editors, and other people connected with the New York entertainment and publishing worlds. Nearby, overlooking Long Island Sound, were the magnificent estates of wealthy business tycoons.[31]

Similarly, Gatsby's parties within *The Great Gatsby* also features famous people whom Gatsby tries to use to impress the Buchanans. As Fitzgerald writes,

> "Perhaps you know that lady," Gatsby indicated a gorgeous, scarcely human orchid of a woman who sat in state under a white-plum tree. Tom and Daisy stared, with that peculiarly unreal feeling that accompanies the recognition of a hitherto ghostly celebrity of the movies.

"She's lovely," said Daisy.

"The man bending over her is her director." [32]

Thus, Fitzgerald's descriptions of the elaborate parties and famous attendees at the Gatsby mansion were partly autobiographical.

Further, Fitzgerald relied on the accounts of his partygoing friends, especially after he had moved to France. In fact, knowing that Fitzgerald was interested in these accounts, his closest friends went out of their way to provide him with descriptions. One such "Gatsby-like" account was provided by Ring Lardner, a close friend and a literary contemporary:

> On the Fourth of July, Ed Wynn gave a fireworks display at his new estate in the Grenwolde division. After the children had been sent home, everybody got pie-eyed [drunk] and I never enjoyed a night so much. All the Great Neck professionals did their stuff, the former chorus girls danced, Blanch Ring kissed me and sang, etc. The party lasted through the next day and wound up next evening at Tom Meighan's where the principal entertainment was provided by Lila Lee and another dame, who did some very funny imitations (really funny) in the moonlight on the tennis court. We would ask them to imitate Houdini, or Leon Errol, or Will Rogers, or Elsie Janis; the imitations were all the same, consisting of an aesthetic dance which ended with an unaesthetic fall onto the tennis courts. [33]

Public Personalities

But the fast-paced, party atmosphere was not the only source Fitzgerald used to create an accurate picture of well-to-do 1920s life. He also relied on another contemporary resource: newspapers. Newspapers and other printed publications were the primary sources of information during the Jazz Age. Coupled with the public's fascination with the rich and famous, many of the articles of Fitzgerald's era described people who were very similar to the characters of *The Great Gatsby*.

Almost every major newspaper during this time had society pages that included the rotogravure sections, illustrated supplements that featured movie stars, stage personalities, sports figures, and other celebrities. Fitzgerald relied extensively on these society pages. As Piper explains, "Almost every Sunday the society columns and rotogravure sections of the New York newspapers carried accounts of wealthy young Midwesterners like the Buchanans who had moved to Long Island to enjoy the yachting, polo and other expensive pastimes of the very rich."[34]

Fitzgerald did not try to hide this influence within his novel. The novel's narrator, Nick Carraway, refers to the rotogravure sections when he realizes that he has heard of Jordan Baker before meeting her. As Carraway comments, "I knew now why her face was familiar—its pleasing contemptuous expression had looked out at me from many rotogravure pictures of the sporting life of Asheville and Hot Springs and Palm Beach."[35]

Indeed, Fitzgerald even admitted to using specific people from the newspapers as models for his characters. One such person was Tommy Hitchcock, a wealthy investment banker who was the best polo player of his generation in the United States during the 1920s. Hitchcock was, of course, one of the models for the wealthy polo player who would be Jay Gatsby's principal antagonist, Tom Buchanan. Whereas the rotogravure sections provided models for the likes of Tom and Daisy Buchanan and Jordan Baker, quite another kind of article lent itself to the formation of Jay Gatsby, the novel's protagonist.

Illegal Enterprises

The Roaring Twenties was also an age of rampant corruption and criminal activity, reports of which appeared regularly within the daily newspapers. In 1919 the U.S. Congress passed the Eighteenth Amendment, or the Volstead Act, which outlawed the manufacture and distribution of alcohol until it was repealed in 1933. Although this law—known as Prohibition—prohibited

Anti-Prohibition parades were held to protest the Eighteenth Amendment.

making and selling alcohol, there was no shortage of alcohol for those who could afford it. Instead, an extensive black market thrived. Called bootlegging, it involved either smuggling alcohol from Canada or manufacturing it under the pretense of medicinal use. In addition, the selling and trading of false or stolen bonds or other financial securities was another common illegal practice. Ironically, this practice was often accepted depending on the popularity of the culprit. (Eventually it would contribute to the stock market crash of 1929, giving way to the Great Depression.) Accordingly, a number of true-to-life criminals contributed directly to Fitzgerald's development of Jay Gatsby.

The modern-day stereotype is to think of the criminals of the 1920s as sinister-looking gangsters and underworld mob bosses. Yet evidence suggests that many of the real gangsters were much different than the stereotype suggests. As Herbert Asbury explains in the March 1925 issue of *American Mercury*,

The moving picture and the stage have always portrayed the gangster as a low-browed person with an evilly glinting eye, a plaid cap drawn down over beetling brows and a swagger that in itself is enough to inform the world that here is a man bent on devilment. . . . [Yet] in the main, the really dangerous gangster, the killer, was apt to be something of a dandy.[36]

In fact, these dandies—well-dressed, well-mannered, and sophisticated people—were surprisingly common in New York during the early 1920s. The financial sections of the newspapers regularly reported the mysterious appearance of Gatsby-like figures suddenly emerging from the West with millions of dollars. One such figure was George Remus, whose real-life exploits help explain the connection between Gatsby's pharmaceutical business and Tom Buchanan's claim that Gatsby was a bootlegger. As critic and historian Thomas H. Pauly states,

In 1920 George Remus was a small-time criminal lawyer who purchased a distillery for medicinal spirits in order to circumvent the recently passed Volstead Act. Though today's readers are often confused by the connection between Gatsby's bootlegging and his drugstores, Fitzgerald was merely registering the widespread exploitation of pharmacies' exemption from Prohibition law due to the large quantities of alcohol used in their prescriptions. Remus' success was to make drug stores as well known for alcohol as speakeasies. Within four years, he controlled fourteen distilleries, a sprawling network of pharmacies and some 3,000 employees. He had cornered one-seventh of the national market for medicinal alcohol and realized a gross income of some $25 million.[37]

Well-to-do criminals who specialized in other sorts of crimes were just as popular and prominent. Surprisingly, it was often their popularity that allowed them to escape harsh treatment by the law even when their guilt was established. Piper describes one such case:

A typical example was Charles Victor Bob, who turned up on Wall Street from Colorado, claiming to be the owner of tin mines in South America and copper mines in Canada. He spent money like water, throwing lavish parties for Broadway celebrities who had never heard of him before, and selling gilt-edged mining securities. He was finally indicted on a six-million dollar mail fraud charge, but, in spite of the evidence, three successive juries refused to convict him. So far as the twenties were concerned, anyone as rich, colorful, and successful as Charles Victor Bob deserved a better fate than jail. [38]

In Fitzgerald's era, the most criminal individuals could also be the most rich, which often meant an unheard-of popularity and immunity to legal restrictions. These realities of the 1920s criminal world were used by Fitzgerald as a backdrop for the creation of the seemingly innocent and untouchable Jay Gatsby.

The Fuller-McGee Case

Perhaps no one historical case had a more profound impact on Fitzgerald's creation of Gatsby than the Fuller-McGee case of 1922, which involved the Great Neck resident Edward M. Fuller. In fact, Fitzgerald admitted to Max Perkins that he had studied the Fuller case until he felt that he knew his character, Jay Gatsby, better than he knew his own child.

Like Gatsby, Fuller emerged in New York as if out of nowhere. In 1916 he appeared as the head of his own brokerage firm, E. M. Fuller and Company. Shortly thereafter, Fuller was mentioned in the society sections "as one of a fashionable set that included Gertrude Vanderbilt, Charles A. Stoneham, the owner of the New York Giants baseball team, and Walter B. Silkworth, prominent clubman and president of the Consolidated Exchange." [39] Further, like Gatsby, he quickly established himself as a wealthy and unique Great Neck resident. Notably, he was the first person to commute via private airplane to Atlantic City during the horse-racing season.

But Fuller achieved a different kind of popularity when his company went bankrupt with $6 million in debt on June 22, 1922. As Piper describes,

Fuller and his vice-president, William F. McGee were indicted on a dozen charges including the running of a "bucket-shop," meaning illegal gambling with customer's funds. It took four trials to finally convict Fuller. (The second trial ended in a mistrial as the key witness disappeared, and during the third another key witness was kidnapped by one of Fuller's attorneys and a second [attorney] tried to bribe a jurist.) In the end, both Fuller and McGee received five years each in Sing-Sing [prison], but were able to arrange for the lesser sentence of 12-months for "good behavior."[40]

What makes the connection between the Fuller-McGee case and Gatsby even more striking is that Fuller was known to have close relations with the renowned gambler Arnold Rothstein (although the exact nature of this relationship was never truly clarified in the Fuller-McGee trials). Rothstein—who writer Stanley Walker describes as "the walking bank, the pawnbroker, the fugitive, unhealthy man who sidled along doorways"[41]—provided the model for Gatsby's business partner, Meyer Wolfsheim.

Rothstein, like Wolfsheim, was reputedly involved in a number of criminal activities. He was suspected of operating illegal gambling houses, selling stolen gems, owning brothels, and operating a profitable bootlegging business. Rothstein was thought to have fixed the 1919 World Series, although no conclusive evidence was ever brought against him. Likewise, Wolfsheim is also suspected of this in *The Great Gatsby*. As Gatsby explains to Carraway, "'Meyer Wolfsheim? . . . He's a gambler.' Gatsby hesitated, then added coolly: 'He's the man who fixed the World Series back in 1919.'"[42] Further, Rothstein's main source of income during the 1920s had an even more direct relationship to Gatsby's activities within Fitzgerald's novel. As Pauly describes,

Though Rothstein was to reap handsome profits from Prohibition, his emergence in the 1920's as the most important underworld figure of New York City owed more to an involvement with stolen bonds like the ones Gatsby is pedaling at the time of his death. During the same year as the World Series fix, Jules "Nicky" Arnstein, a long-time gambling friend of Rothstein's, stole some $5 million worth of Liberty bonds from vulnerable errand boys relaying them between brokerage houses and banks. . . . Significantly, these bonds were never recovered; meanwhile Liberty bonds played a role in several important Rothstein deals. Rothstein's take from these bonds vastly exceeded his return from the fixed Series and was perhaps his single most lucrative venture. Indeed, Tom Buchanan's sources appear more reliable in his characterization of Gatsby's drug store chain as "just small change" compared to his stolen bonds. [43]

In fact, Fitzgerald alludes to Rothstein's life indirectly within *The Great Gatsby* during Carraway's first conversation with Wolfsheim when Wolfsheim reflects on the restaurant the Metropole: "'The old Metropole,' brooded Mr. Wolfsheim gloomily. 'Filled with faces dead and gone. Filled with friends now gone forever. I can't forget so long as I live the night they shot Rosy Rosenthal there.'" [44] In real life, Rothstein's criminal career was almost compromised by the gangster-style execution of one of his close associates, Herman Rosenthal. And with this allusion to Rosenthal, Fitzgerald not only admits the connection with Rothstein but also to Fuller as both were direct models for the plot and characters of *The Great Gatsby*.

The Failing American Dream

Fitzgerald's references to both the rotogravure sections as well as contemporary criminals not only reflect the realities of life within the 1920s but also the failing of the American dream. The idea of the American dream is that any person can succeed if he or she works hard enough. Fitzgerald's Jay Gatsby would, in one way,

Flappers were free-spirited women of the 1920s and represented the prosperity and good times of the decade.

seem to meet this criteria; Gatsby accumulated his wealth on his own without the advantage of a wealthy upbringing. Yet Gatsby's methods for gaining his wealth were of illegal means. Likewise, the 1920s was an era of prosperity, much of it illegally gained. Through the death of Jay Gatsby, Fitzgerald suggests that the consequences of achieving the American dream through illegal and hurtful means has a very negative result. According to Piper,

> The files of the Fuller-McGee case prove concretely what *The Great Gatsby* implies indirectly: that society leaders, financial tycoons, politicians, magistrates, pimps, jurors, lawyers, baseball players, bond salesmen, debutantes, and prostitutes—all shared in some degree the responsibility for Gatsby's fate.[45]

Fitzgerald saw the illusive reality of the 1920s even before it resulted in the Great Depression. *The Great Gatsby* is a critical look at the 1920s version of the American dream: the quest for quick riches and quicker fun. Gatsby, like the real-life people of Fitzgerald's era, gives himself over to the pursuit of wealth as a way to actualize his dreams.

Fitzgerald acknowledges how difficult it is to understand the appeal of wealth or the ideals it represents. Nowhere is this more apparent than in Carraway's reaction to Gatsby's explanation of his love for Daisy. For Gatsby, Daisy is the personification of wealth; because of this, the attainment of Daisy symbolizes Gatsby's own success at achieving the American dream. Yet Carraway cannot find a good way to explain this connection. As Carraway says in response to Gatsby's explanation of his love for Daisy,

> Through all he said, even through his appalling sentimentality, I was reminded of something—an elusive rhythm, a fragment of lost words, that I had heard somewhere a long time ago. For a moment a phrase tried to take shape in my mouth and my lips parted like a dumb man's, as though there was more struggling upon them than a wisp of startled air. But they made no sound, and what I had almost remembered was uncommunicable forever.[46]

Likewise, Fitzgerald's attempt to come to terms with the world in which he lived seems to be equally as difficult to mutter. As Marius Bewley explains,

> *The Great Gatsby* is an exploration of the American dream as it exists in a corrupt period, and it is an attempt to determine that concealed boundary that divides the reality from the illusions. The illusions seem more real than the reality itself. . . . In Gatsby's America, the reality is undefined to itself. It is inarticulate and frustrated.[47]

In this way, *The Great Gatsby* becomes a critical look at the reality of the American dream versus the ideal. For although it is the ideal, as symbolized by Daisy, that leads Gatsby on his quest for riches and prestige, it is the reality of his situation that leads him to his final doom. The death of Gatsby is therefore a final critique on the value of the American dream in the 1920s.

CHAPTER THREE

Wealth, Love, and Tragedy

T he *Great Gatsby* is the 1920s story of the final summer of the wealthy Jay Gatsby, as told by Nick Carraway, his neighbor and eventual friend. Within the narrative, Carraway tells of Gatsby's rise to personal fortune through criminal practices. Yet he also provides a sensitive insight into the romantic ideals of Gatsby, especially with respect to his pursuit of the now-married Daisy Buchanan. The tragic result of this pursuit is the death of Gatsby himself as he becomes a victim of his own dreams. His murder results from the careless attitudes of the elitist class, of which Gatsby desperately wishes to be a part.

Gatsby's story, however, also becomes the story of the young Nick Carraway. Because Carraway is the narrator of the novel, his changing opinions of Gatsby's dream-chasing reflect Carraway's own change in character throughout the progression of the novel. Carraway realizes that Gatsby's dilemma is an attempt to reconcile love with the materialistic

Gatsby's futile pursuit of Daisy is the cause of his downfall.

hopes for greater wealth. Carraway, too, hopes to reconcile emotional ideals, like love, with the harsh realities of life, such as the ghastly fates of Myrtle Wilson and Gatsby. Carraway's situation is therefore similar to Gatsby's because they both attempt to reconcile the power and prestige of money with the moral dilemmas that great wealth can bring. In this way, both Gatsby's and Carraway's struggles represent the problematic realities of the 1920s.

Chapter One: The Buchanans and Jordan Baker

The story begins when Carraway outlines the events that brought him to Long Island Sound. He introduces the layout of Long Island Sound, which notably includes the geography and social separation of East and West Egg, a division between the "new money" of those who became rich thanks to the affluence of the 1920s and the "old money" of families who had been rich for generations.

Carraway then tells of an evening dinner party at the mansion of his cousin Daisy and her husband, Tom Buchanan, in West Egg. The dinner was held in Carraway's honor since he had only recently arrived to Long Island Sound. On his arrival, Carraway has a brief conversation with Tom on the porch. During the conversation Carraway is intimidated by his former schoolmate's physique and social status, but he is also critical of Tom's elitism.

Once inside, Carraway is greeted by Daisy. She in turn introduces him to Jordan Baker, who Carraway later recognizes as a famous amateur athlete who had recently been involved in an unpleasant scandal, the details of which he cannot remember. After their introductions, Baker asks Carraway if he knows Jay Gatsby, and Daisy is unexplainably shocked by this question.

During dinner, Tom leaves the table to answer a phone call; he is hurriedly followed by Daisy. While they are away, Baker tells Carraway that the call is from Tom's mistress, who lives in New York. In response, Daisy, in an after-dinner private conversation about her toddler daughter with Carraway, confesses her belief that the best thing a girl can be is a "beautiful fool."

When Carraway returns home, he glimpses Gatsby in his yard, which is next door to Carraway's own. Gatsby seems to be trembling, and his arms are eerily stretched seaward toward a green light across the bay. Sensing that it would be inappropriate, Carraway does not call out to his new neighbor and instead goes directly to bed.

Chapter Two: The Mistress of Tom Buchanan

Not many days after the dinner, Carraway and Tom travel to Manhattan together via train. Tom insists that they both exit the train so that Carraway can meet Tom's mistress, Myrtle Wilson. They descend into Queens, an area Carraway describes as a "valley of ashes,"[48] and walk to the garage and filling station owned by George Wilson. Over the garage a billboard of spectacled eyes ominously advertises the services of Dr. T. J. Eckleburg. Tom and George briefly discusses the possible sale of Tom's car, but it soon becomes apparent that the proposed deal is only a ruse so that Tom can tell Myrtle to meet him on the next train to Manhattan.

Once in Manhattan, the three go to Myrtle and Tom's New York apartment. Myrtle's friends the McKees and her sister, Catherine, are invited over. Over drinks, Catherine discusses rumors about the sources of Gatsby's money and the prospects of Tom and Myrtle getting married, something that Carraway knows to be unlikely. The discussion provokes Myrtle to discuss her mistake of marrying George Wilson, a man whom she believes to be below her socially.

During the course of the evening, the entire party proceeds to drink heavily. Myrtle and Tom have a drunken argument over whether Myrtle has the right to say Daisy's name. To rebuke Tom, Myrtle chants Daisy's name, and Tom hits her and breaks her nose. This provokes the drunken Carraway to leave the apartment and head home to Long Island Sound. He arrives at the Manhattan station to wait for his train at four in the morning.

Chapter Three: Gatsby's Party

On a Saturday morning not long thereafter, Carraway receives an invitation to Jay Gatsby's party that evening. However, Carraway

Large, elaborate, and wild parties are a common occurrence at Gatsby's home.

explains that this was not the first party Gatsby had hosted. In fact, Gatsby puts on a huge party at least every two weeks, each of which requires elaborate preparations in order to provide for the hundreds of guests, including an orchestra and cocktails and buffet tables that are constantly restocked.

Later that evening, at the party, Carraway runs into Jordan Baker for the first time since their meeting at the Buchanans' dinner party. While they are becoming reacquainted, they are approached by Jordan's acquaintance, Lucille, who is in the company of friends; they discuss the romantic rumors that surround Gatsby, including the tale that he killed a man. The conversation ends with the serving of supper. At Baker's invitation, Carraway joins her at the table reserved for the residents of East Egg, but they quickly retreat to the mansion to look for their host.

Inside Gatsby's mansion Carraway and Baker find only a bespectacled older man in the library. He raves to them that the library contains real books. Unable to find Gatsby inside, Baker and Carraway go back to the garden, where Carraway talks of the Great War with a man his own age; eventually, Carraway discovers that he has inadvertently met Jay Gatsby. The two talk only a bit longer, and Gatsby ends their conversation with an invitation to ride on his hydroplane the next morning.

Later, Gatsby's butler approaches Baker and asks for a private conversation between her and Gatsby. Baker leaves; when she returns, she tells Carraway that Gatsby had told her something ridiculous, but she will not disclose what. When she departs, Carraway remains in order to thank Gatsby for the invitation. After saying good night, he walks down the front walk and witnesses a traffic jam in the driveway caused by an exceedingly drunk driver who drove his car into a ditch.

On leaving Gatsby's, Carraway breaks from the narrative to explain that his summer was much more than simply the three days he had so far revealed in the novel. He gives an account of his average doings both in Long Island and in Manhattan. He also confesses that he spends an increasing amount of time with Jordan Baker. He goes on to give an account of driving with Baker, in which he accuses her of being careless. Carraway closes the chapter with an admission of an affection for Baker that causes him to break off a relationship with an unnamed girl in the Midwest. This provokes Carraway to confess that he is one of the few honest people he has ever known.

Chapter Four: Gatsby's Request

Several weeks later, near the end of July, Gatsby drives his expensive car into the driveway of Carraway's house at nine in the morning. It is the first time that Gatsby has called on Carraway, although Carraway admits that he has attended two of his parties, rode on his hydroplane, and used his private beach. When Carraway meets Gatsby in the driveway, Gatsby offers to drive him into the city and insists that they have lunch together.

During the drive, Gatsby tells Carraway not to believe all of the rumors of his origins and explains that he is from San Francisco, that his parents are dead, and that he received his education at Oxford. Gatsby also tells him of his involvement in the war. Although Carraway is initially inclined not to believe him, he is convinced of the accuracy of Gatsby's claims when Gatsby shows him, while still in the car, a medal from the war and a photo of himself while at Oxford. After gaining Carraway's trust, Gatsby informs him that Jordan Baker will ask him a favor on behalf of Gatsby later that afternoon.

At lunch Gatsby introduces Carraway to his business partner, Meyer Wolfsheim. Carraway is shocked to discover that Wolfsheim's cufflinks are made of human teeth. When Wolfsheim parts, Gatsby informs Carraway that Wolfsheim is the notorious gambler who had fixed the 1919 World Series. Later, Carraway notices Tom Buchanan at the same club; he tries to introduce him to Gatsby, but Gatsby has already made a hasty retreat.

Later that afternoon Carraway and Baker meet for tea, and she issues Gatsby's request: that Carraway arrange for a meeting between Daisy and Gatsby. Baker explains that a love affair once existed between the two before Daisy's marriage and that Gatsby had moved to Long Island Sound with the express purpose of seeing Daisy. She also tells him of Daisy's drunken state the night of her wedding-party dinner, during which she tried to call off her marriage to Tom in memory of Gatsby. Afterward, Baker and Carraway kiss.

Chapter Five: A Secret Rendezvous

Carraway returns home that same evening to find Gatsby's empty mansion completely lit up. Gatsby crosses his lawn to speak with Carraway, and Carraway informs him that he has spoken with Jordan Baker. In an effort to repay Carraway for his assistance, Gatsby seeks to involve Carraway in a moneymaking deal, but Carraway declines out of pride.

The next morning Carraway invites Daisy Buchanan to tea; he advises her not to bring her husband. On the day of the tea, Gatsby arrives at Carraway's at the appointed time; he is obviously nervous. Daisy arrives shortly thereafter. After some initial awkwardness, Carraway leaves Gatsby and Daisy alone together. Carraway returns sometime later to find Daisy crying but happy.

The three agree to go for a tour of Gatsby's mansion, which culminates with Gatsby showing off some expensive shirts. Gatsby also explains to Daisy that the green light is at the end of the dock of the Buchanans' estate. Carraway comments on a portrait hanging in Gatsby's bedroom, and Gatsby informs him that it is Dan Cody, an old friend now dead. Gatsby and Daisy speak together with an increasing intimacy until Carraway, feeling out of place, attempts to leave. Neither Gatsby nor Daisy would hear of it until another person, the boarder Klipspringer, joins them and plays on the piano. As Carraway makes his exit, he notices Gatsby's bewildered appearance, as if he cannot comprehend his current happiness.

Chapter Six: Gatsby's Past

Carraway begins the chapter by relating the truth of Gatsby's origins to the reader, the details of which Carraway admits to learning only much later. Gatsby started life as James Gatz, the son of failed farmers. When Gatsby was in his late teens, while combing the beaches of Lake Superior, he saw a yacht moored in the distance. He borrowed a rowboat and headed toward the yacht under the pretense of informing its captain that severe winds were known to capsize moored boats in that area of the lake. The captain, Dan Cody, was a wealthy fifty-year-old who had made his money from mining. James Gatz immediately introduced himself as Jay Gatsby, a name he had already invented for himself in an effort to escape his poor upbringing. Cody took Gatsby into his service. When Cody died, he left Gatsby some money, but Gatsby never received it due to a legal device used by Ella Kaye, Cody's mistress. Although Gatsby was again penniless, he had succeeded in developing the persona of Jay Gatsby.

With this explained, Carraway reveals that he had not been to see Gatsby for several weeks because he had been spending time with Jordan Baker. Then, on a Sunday, Carraway stops over for a drink. To his and Gatsby's surprise, Tom Buchanan, in the company of a man named Sloane and his lady friend, also pay Gatsby a visit. After a brief conversation in which Gatsby acknowledges that he and Tom have met once before, Gatsby admits to know-ing Daisy. Hospitably, Gatsby invites them to stay for dinner. The lady responds by asking if Gatsby and Carraway would dine with her instead. Carraway perceives this as a token gesture, but Gatsby does not. Tom, Sloane, and Sloane's lady friend leave without Gatsby when he goes upstairs for his jacket.

The following weekend Tom arrives at Gatsby's party with Daisy. Neither Tom nor Daisy are impressed with the party, despite the many famous people in attendance. Tom threatens to inquire what Gatsby truly does for a living, and Carraway rises to Gatsby's defense. The evening ends with an intimate conversation between Carraway and Gatsby in which Gatsby proclaims his belief that one can repeat the past. He confesses to Carraway the story of his and Daisy's first kiss, five years previous. Carraway is touched, although he cannot put words to his emotions.

Chapter Seven: A Fatal Wreck

As the general curiosity about Gatsby's origins and sources of wealth intensifies, Carraway notices that the habitual weekend revelers are being turned away from Gatsby's mansion. Concerned, Carraway tries to pay Gatsby a visit, but he, too, is turned away by an unfamiliar butler. The next day Gatsby phones Carraway and informs him that Daisy comes over most after-noons, so he replaced his servants with people who would not gossip. Gatsby also informs him that Daisy would like Carraway to go to her house for lunch the next day.

The following day Carraway and Gatsby go to the Buchanans', where they find Daisy and Jordan Baker. Tom is on the phone to George Wilson about the car Wilson hopes to buy. After the conversation ends, Tom enters the room but leaves again at Daisy's request for him to make drinks. In Tom's absence, Daisy confesses her love to Gatsby and kisses him. A nurse enters the room with Daisy and Tom's child; Daisy points out that the child looks like her and not Tom.

When Tom returns with the drinks, Daisy suggests that they go into Manhattan. She then comments on how cool Gatsby looks, and Carraway notes that at the moment Tom realizes that Daisy loves Gatsby. In a side comment, Gatsby confesses to Carraway that he cannot say anything about his love for Daisy to Tom while in Tom's house.

Before leaving for Manhattan, Gatsby suggests that they take his car, but Tom insists that he drive Gatsby's and that Gatsby drive his coupé. To Tom's dissatisfaction, Daisy insists on riding with Gatsby; Carraway and Baker accompany Tom. In the car, Tom admits that he has had Gatsby investigated and that he does not believe that Gatsby truly attended Oxford. Gatsby's car is low on gas, so Tom stops at George Wilson's garage. An ill George informs Tom that he and Myrtle will be moving west. Carraway realizes that George knows that his wife is having an affair, but he does not suspect Tom. He sees Myrtle looking jealously out of the window at Baker and perceives that she must think that Baker is Daisy.

Both cars meet in Manhattan, and they agree on the idea of taking a room at the Plaza Hotel. In the hotel room, Tom chastises Daisy for complaining about the heat. Gatsby rises to her defense. On the defensive, Tom chides Gatsby for his use of the phrase "old sport" and then voices his suspicion that Gatsby never attended Oxford. Gatsby explains that he attended Oxford for five months after fighting in the Great War.

Rebuffed, Tom confronts Gatsby on the subject of his affection for Daisy. Gatsby declares that he and Daisy love each other and that she has never loved Tom. An argument ensues in which both Gatsby and Tom challenge Daisy to admit that she had never loved Tom. Daisy tells Gatsby that he wants too much. Gatsby recovers from Daisy's remark and tells Tom that Daisy is leaving him. In response to Gatsby's assertion, Tom ridicules the social standing of Gatsby by revealing that a portion of Gatsby's fortune was obtained as Wolfsheim's partner in bootlegging and that he is currently involved in an even more secretive deal.

Since Tom feels that he has won the argument, he sends Daisy and Gatsby home in Gatsby's car. Baker and Carraway remain with Tom. On the way home the occupants of Tom's car come upon the scene of a hit-and-run accident. Tom discovers that Myrtle Wilson was killed in the accident by a yellow car that matches the description of Gatsby's. Tom calls Gatsby a coward for not stopping his car. When they arrive at the Buchanans', Carraway declines Baker's invitation to come inside because he is struck by her lack of emotion over the death of Myrtle.

While waiting outside for a taxi, he finds Gatsby hiding in the bushes. In the course of their conversation, Gatsby admits that Daisy had been driving the car. As a favor to the curious Gatsby, Carraway peers through the Buchanans' window to see Daisy and Tom talking intimately. He leaves, but Gatsby remains as he is falsely convinced that Tom might try to harm Daisy.

Chapter Eight: Revenge

The next day Carraway awakes early in the morning to the sound of Gatsby returning home. Carraway approaches him in his driveway and advises him to go away for a while since the police will trace the car. Gatsby refuses. The two have breakfast together at Gatsby's house, during which Gatsby tells Carraway of his last days with Daisy before going to the war and of a letter he received while at Oxford that told him of her marriage to Tom. After breakfast Carraway reluctantly leaves for work. Just before departing he tells Gatsby that he is a better person than either the Buchanans or Jordan Baker. Later that day Baker calls Carraway to invite him for afternoon tea, but he bluntly declines. He then attempts to call Gatsby, but the line is busy because Gatsby had the operator reserve it for a call from Daisy. However, the call never comes.

Carraway then narrates what occurred at George Wilson's garage the previous day. Wilson had found a new leash for the dog Tom had bought Myrtle, and he surmised that his wife was having an affair. When he confronted her, she admitted to having a lover but justified her unfaithfulness as a result of Wilson's weakness. After Myrtle had been run over by the car, Wilson assumed

Nick learns that Gatsby had been in the pool when George Wilson fatally shot him.

that the driver of the car and Myrtle's lover were the same person. The next morning Wilson traced the car to Gatsby.

That afternoon, after work, Carraway goes to Gatsby's home, where he discovers both Gatsby's and Wilson's dead bodies. Carraway explains that Wilson shot Gatsby while he was in the swimming pool and then shot himself.

Chapter Nine: The Funeral

Shortly thereafter, Carraway explains that he is the one who tends to Gatsby's funeral arrangements. He also confesses to the reader that he had called Daisy after finding Gatsby's body only to learn that she and Tom had left permanently that afternoon. The day after Gatsby's death, Carraway sends Gatsby's butler to New York with a letter for Wolfsheim. However, he responds by explaining that he is unable to assist Carraway with the funeral and that he knows of no family. While trying to locate Gatsby's family, Carraway receives a call from Chicago that he hopes to be from Daisy; instead, it is from a man called Slagle. Slagle mistakes Carraway for Gatsby, and in the confusion, he betrays the source of Gatsby's income: selling stolen or forged bonds.

The third day after Gatsby's death, Carraway receives a telegram from Henry C. Gatz, Gatsby's father, which asks to postpone the funeral until he arrives. When he arrives, Carraway shows him Gatsby's body. Afterward, Gatz expounds on how great a man his son would have become had he lived longer. Later, Gatz shows Carraway a ragged copy of *Hopalong Cassidy* in which Gatsby, as a child, had penned his schedule and resolves. These show Gatsby to be, even as a child, a person interested in reinventing himself.

On the day of the funeral, not a single person other than Carraway, Gatz, and the servants show up. However, when the procession arrives at the cemetery, the man with the owl-eye glasses arrives. After the funeral he expresses outrage at the lack of attendance as it is clear that those who attended Gatsby's parties were not truly friends.

Because of his disgust with the events that led to Gatsby's death, Carraway decides to leave the East and return to the Midwest. Before he leaves, Carraway meets with Jordan Baker one last time. She accuses him of being a careless person for leaving her. Carraway tells her that he would have been lying to himself had he stayed with her. Carraway also reveals how he stumbled across Tom much later that year. When they meet, Tom, at Carraway's prodding, admits to telling George Wilson where Gatsby lived. Although Carraway is unable to forgive Tom for his role in the murder of Gatsby, he also realizes that Tom believes himself to be entirely justified because he still thinks that Gatsby was the driver of the car that had struck Myrtle.

In his final reflections, which are addressed to the reader, Carraway accuses the Buchanans of being careless with their lives and spoiled by the power of their money. He then relates his last night at West Egg, during which he reflected on Gatsby's belief that past opportunities, like the love of Daisy, could be recaptured in the future. Carraway concludes that all dreams of the future are like Gatsby's—they are all intimately connected to missed opportunities of the past.

CHAPTER FOUR

The Characters of *The Great Gatsby*

A lthough *The Great Gatsby* is primarily the tragic story of Jay Gatsby, it is narrated by Nick Carraway. Thus, the reader is limited to Carraway's impressions of Gatsby and the other characters in Gatsby's life. Therefore, the reader is asked to have faith in Carraway's own declaration of honesty, for it is only through his eyes and his experiences that the story is told. Sometimes this limits the reader's knowledge of the characters since Carraway does not always provide the full name or any name, as is the case of the man with the owl-eye glasses. Carraway's penchant for detail and his willingness to criticize himself as well as the other people who played a role in Gatsby's tragic history, however, allow for a profound and often complicated insight into the characters of *The Great Gatsby*.

Jordan Baker

Jordan Baker is the girlhood friend of Daisy Buchanan and, for most of the novel, a developing love interest for the narrator. As a wealthy young woman under the charge of an elderly aunt, Baker spends her time either at the houses of her elite group of friends, like the Buchanans, or on amateur golf tours.

Carraway initially finds Baker's independence and even her carelessness appealing. Yet, with the accidental murder of Myrtle Wilson, Carraway reevaluates his affection for the careless Baker because she is apparently so removed from Myrtle's death. As critic Susan Resnesck Parr explains,

> When Nick accuses her of being a rotten driver, she justifies her own behavior on the grounds that other people are careful. When Nick warns her that she might meet "somebody just as careless as yourself," Jordan responds easily: "I hope I never do . . . I hate careless people. That's why I like you." But when Jordan becomes associated in Nick's mind with Daisy and Tom and the chaos and destruction they create, he moves away from the relationship. For her part, whatever the anger and disappointment, Jordan maintains her pose. . . . But even though Jordan is able to create a personality made up of a series of gestures, her life ultimately seems both purposeless and empty.[49]

Carraway's ultimate disgust with Baker's nonchalance is made clear by his treatment of her during their last meeting. Although it hurts him to leave Baker because he believes he is still somewhat in love with her, he cannot bring himself to continue the relationship.

In respite, Baker accuses Carraway of being as careless as he accuses her of being. He responds that he is too old to be able to lie to himself any longer. As Carraway narrates, "'I'm thirty,' I said. 'I'm five years too old to lie to myself and call it honor.' She didn't answer. Angry, and half in love with her, and tremendously sorry, I turned away."[50] Baker, therefore, represents Carraway's initial attraction to the world of the wealthy elite as well as his eventual repulsion and dismissal of the rich and careless.

Daisy Buchanan

Daisy Buchanan is the wife of wealthy Tom Buchanan and is Nick Carraway's second cousin. Beautiful and quick-witted, she is also the reason for Gatsby's arrival at Long Island Sound and eventually the cause of Gatsby's demise. Before marrying Tom, Daisy was courted by Gatsby just before he was shipped to Europe to fight in World War I. However, Daisy married Tom before Gatsby could return. She did not forget entirely about Gatsby, though, and after he returns the two have an affair.

Importantly, because Gatsby had yet to make his fortune when he first met her, Daisy becomes the symbol of what he could have attained had he been wealthy. In other words, Gatsby tries to relive his youth before the war through the attainment of Daisy. But Daisy is unable to live up to the perfect

Though Daisy is married to Tom Buchanan, she still has feelings for Gatsby.

image Gatsby has created for her. As literary critic Elizabeth Kaspar Aldrich explains,

> Daisy "in life" cannot sustain Gatsby's faith in and demands on her as a symbol [of Gatsby's desires]. This is the subject of the work . . . [the] translation of living [woman] to symbol. In *Gatsby* the translation is of Daisy whose history and affective life are "only personal" to the inhuman green light [which represents Daisy] to which Gatsby stretches forth his arms.[51]

Daisy is therefore caught between her own desires and weaknesses and Gatsby's idealized vision of her. As a result of this conflict, she retreats from Gatsby at the end of the novel. When Gatsby confronts Tom with the reality of his love for Daisy, she is not able to share Gatsby's idealized vision of their relationship. As she explains in *The Great Gatsby,* "'Oh, you want too much!' she cried to Gatsby. 'I love you now—isn't that enough? I can't help what's past.' She began to sob helplessly. 'I did love him once—but I loved you too.'" [52]

After accidentally running down Myrtle Wilson while driving Gatsby's car, Daisy is shaken by the cold reality of her inadvertent murder. She returns to her husband and his money, leaving Gatsby to fend for himself.

Tom Buchanan

Tom Buchanan is the husband of Daisy and a former Yale football star and university contemporary of Nick Carraway. Tom's abundant wealth allows him to afford to have polo ponies brought out to East Egg on a whim. Tom is physically strong and intimidating, yet Carraway pegs him as an intellectual inferior who struggles with regurgitated ideas such as his explanation of *The History of Colored Peoples* during Carraway's first dinner at his house.

Tom represents the elite class, to which Gatsby hopelessly aspires throughout the novel. He was able to marry Daisy because he possesses incredible wealth. In fact, this same elitism motivates Tom to aid Gatsby's murderer. Although Tom has had numerous affairs, he will not tolerate a man with a common background like Gatsby challenging him over Daisy. He is also resentful of the illegal manner by which Gatsby established his personal fortune because it is in stark contrast to the old money provided Tom Buchanan by his birth. As Tom says when Gatsby claims that he and Daisy are going to marry, "'She's not leaving me!' Tom's words suddenly leaned down over Gatsby. 'Certainly not for a common swindler who'd have to steal the ring he put on her finger.'" [53]

When the vengeful George Wilson shows up at Tom's mansion in East Egg, Tom directs him to Gatsby's home, which results in Gatsby's murder. As a result of Tom's lack of regard for Gatsby's life, he also becomes the embodiment of the carelessness that Carraway comes to abhor by the novel's end. When Carraway sees Tom for the last time on a New York street, Tom's admission to abetting Wilson's murder causes Carraway to severely indict both

Tom and the elitist class that he represents as people who "smashed up things and creatures and then retreated back into their money or their vast carelessness, or whatever it was that kept them together, and let other people clean up the mess they had made."[54]

Nick Carraway

Although Carraway is not the novel's protagonist, it is with Carraway that the reader is the most intimately associated since he is the story's narrator. Carraway is originally from the Midwest and from a modestly wealthy family. After receiving his education at Yale (with Tom Buchanan), he travels to New York to become a bondsman. He rents a house in West Egg on Long Island Sound, which happens to be next door to Gatsby's mansion and across the bay from his cousin Daisy. Carraway prides himself on his honesty. As he states, "Every one suspects himself of at least one of the cardinal virtues, and this is mine: I am one of the few honest people that I have ever known."[55]

Nick Carraway (right) initially is impressed with the members of the Long Island elite, but later becomes contemptuous of them.

Yet Carraway, too, is caught in the routine carelessness of the Buchanans, as is illustrated when he unwillingly bows to Tom's pressure to accompany him and his lover, Myrtle Wilson, to their Manhattan apartment. Furthermore, Carraway helps arrange the initial meeting between Gatsby and Daisy. And he consistently pursues his relationship with Jordan Baker even though he recognizes that he is not completely in love with her. In fact, Baker embodies the careless mentality that he is later driven to critique.

Much of Carraway's contradictions can be attributed to the difficulty he has discovering what is truly important in a world fettered by careless attitudes and enormous wealth. As Parr explains,

> In some moments, he is hopeful about what the future might hold and is drawn to the excitement which accompanies that change. In other moments, his awareness of human vulnerability overshadows his confidence in life's promise, and so he retreats from whatever situation provoked his anxiety and unhappiness in an effort to exert control and establish a sense of order. That the world around him so often seems chaotic and the people he knows without purpose almost certainly contributes to his ambivalence.[56]

But he is also the only person to appreciate Gatsby, both as Jay Gatsby and James Gatz. Carraway sees the wonder of Gatsby's initial building of his new persona under the tutelage of Dan Cody as well as his persistence at trying to create the future from past opportunities. Furthermore, he is the only one to stick by Gatsby in the end. In fact, he feels more responsible for Gatsby because he is the only one who seems to care about him. This responsibility, however, is also accompanied by a relative respect. As he states to Gatsby the morning after the death of Myrtle Wilson, "'They're a rotten crowd,' I shouted across the lawn. 'You're worth the whole damn bunch put together.'"[57] Indeed, Carraway's dislike for the Buchanans is proportionate to his appreciation of the romantic nature of Jay Gatsby.

Catherine

Catherine is Myrtle Wilson's sister, and she attends the small party at the New York apartment. Her purpose in the novel is twofold. First, she gives voice to Myrtle's dream of becoming the new Mrs. Buchanan. She is convinced that Tom Buchanan means to divorce Daisy and marry her sister instead. Indeed, she tells Carraway that this would have happened already had Daisy not been Catholic and therefore against divorce. Second, she allows Carraway to understand that Tom readily lies to Myrtle to sustain the affair: Daisy is not Catholic. Catherine also appears near the end of the novel to squelch any rumors that Myrtle had known Gatsby. She does not reveal Myrtle's affair with Tom.

Dan Cody

Dan Cody is the fifty-year-old wealthy miner who acted as the catalyst for the formation of James Gatz's new identity as Jay Gatsby. As a young man, full of dreams but poor in pocket, Gatsby had rowed a boat out to Cody's moored yacht, called the *Tuolomee*, to warn him of winds that could endanger his ship. When Gatsby boarded Cody's yacht, Cody asked him a few questions—one of which elicited the brand new name Jay Gatsby. Cody was the first person to recognize the latent potential of James Gatz.

A few days later Cody bought Gatsby a blue coat, six pairs of white duck trousers, and a yachting cap. Later, Cody took Gatsby to the West Indies and the Barbary Coast, where Gatsby became Cody's caretaker because Cody drank excessively (the reason Carraway cites for Gatsby's general abstention from alcohol).

When Cody died, he left Gatsby twenty-five thousand dollars, but Gatsby never received it due to legal manipulations by Cody's lover, Ella Kaye. However, the person that Gatsby became while with Cody was the groomed and debonair personality that Meyer Wolfsheim later found—penniless but self-assured and ambitious.

Jay Gatsby

Jay Gatsby, the protagonist and hero of *The Great Gatsby*, is the former James Gatz, the son of the poor Midwest farmer Henry

C. Gatz. Gatsby was a boy who dreamed of a far more extravagant and sophisticated lifestyle than the one he possessed. From these dreams he constructed the persona of Jay Gatsby, which was allowed to come to life through the meeting of Dan Cody on Lake Superior.

While with Cody, Gatsby constructed a new personality that enticed the interest of Daisy, whom he met just before going overseas to fight as an officer in World War I. To his disappointment, however, Daisy was unwilling to accommodate the length of his stay abroad; in the meantime, she met and married Tom Buchanan. After a decorated military career in which he was promoted to major, Gatsby spent five months attending Oxford University. After he returned to the United States penniless, Gatsby made the acquaintance of Meyer Wolfsheim, who made good use of Gatsby's sophisticated and likable personality: Together they became involved in a number of illegal endeavors, including bootlegging and selling stolen or forged bonds. As a result, Gatsby quickly came into enormous wealth.

Gatsby is a man who believes that he can transform himself by purchasing the appropriate things, such as his mansion, clothes, and car, and by assuming the appropriate mannerisms and gestures. Gatsby believes that if he acts the part of the elite, he will be perceived as being from an upper-class childhood and lifestyle. As Parr explains,

> Gatsby hears the "drums of destiny" as defined by a version of the American dream of success that applies to men. In fact, whereas most young men, according to Nick, in moments of "intimate revelation," tell tales that are in reality plagiaristic, Gatsby goes a step further and actually lives out some of the myths of the culture. In support of his new identity, Gatsby adopts what he believes are the appropriate mannerisms and surrounds himself with what he believes are the right props. He calls other men "Old Sport," drives an expensive, fancy car, and lives in a mansion in West Egg, which, he tells Daisy, he keeps "always

full of interesting people, night and day. People who do interesting things. Celebrated people." He also goes to great lengths to create a sense of authenticity. As Owl-Eyes puts it when he discovers that the books in Gatsby's library are real, "This fella's a regular Belasco. It's a triumph. What thoroughness! What realism!"[58]

This desire for realism leads Gatsby to seek to marry Daisy Buchanan. Marriage to her would mean a marriage into the families of the elite. Thus, Gatsby moves to Long Island Sound in order to win her love. He believes that he can reconstruct the love that should have happened between him and Daisy had he been a wealthy man at the time of their initial romance. As Fitzgerald relates in a conversation between Carraway and Gatsby,

"I wouldn't ask too much of her [Daisy]," I [Carraway] ventured. "You can't repeat the past."

"Can't repeat the past?" he [Gatsby] cried incredulously. "Why of course you can!"

Gatsby believes he can re-create his relationship with Daisy by pursuing the lifestyle of a wealthy man.

He looked around him wildly, as if the past were lurking here in the shadow of his house, just out of reach of his hand.

"I'm going to fix everything just the way it was before," he said, nodding determinedly. "She'll see."[59]

As a romantic, Gatsby believes he can re-create the past because of his affection for it. It is his faith in romanticism that allows him to momentarily succeed in winning Daisy, but it is also the cause of his demise.

When Daisy accidentally kills Myrtle Wilson with Gatsby's car, he becomes the target of Wilson's search for the lover of his deceased wife. Yet it is Gatsby's death that protects him from the knowledge that Daisy and Tom Buchanan had already left Long Island Sound. Indeed, in the final pages of the novel, Carraway looks past Gatsby's faults and admires his romantic ideals in contrast with the Buchanans, the cowardly beneficiaries of old money. As such, Gatsby's purpose in the novel is primarily to reflect on the elitist attitudes of 1920s America.

Henry C. Gatz

Henry C. Gatz is Jay Gatsby's father. Although Gatsby told Carraway that his parents were dead, Gatz reads of his son's death in a Chicago paper and wires to ask that the funeral be postponed until he can arrive. After viewing the body of his deceased son, Gatz speaks with admiration of Gatsby. He believes that Gatsby would one day have been a great man who molded the future of America. Gatz also confesses that Gatsby last visited him two years ago and that he had bought him a house and provided him with some money.

Gatz also shows Carraway the flyleaf of one of Gatsby's childhood books, *Hopalong Cassidy*, on which is printed the young James Gatz's "schedule"—which includes time slots for the practice of good manners and the improving of one's mind—and a much-handled photo of Gatsby's mansion. Gatz expresses latent admiration for this schedule as a testament to his son's success.

Gatz laughs as he recalls that he once beat his son for admonishing his father for eating like a hog. Afterward, as Carraway relates, "[Henry C. Gatz] was reluctant to close the book, reading each item aloud and then looking eagerly at me. I think he rather expected me to copy down the list for my own use."[60]

Gatz reveals aspects of Gatsby that allow Carraway to come to a new and deeper understanding of the person who was Jay Gatsby. As a result of these insights, Carraway also gains a new appreciation for Gatsby's perseverance, which ended with his death at Long Island Sound.

Ella Kaye

Ella Kaye was Dan Cody's mistress. When Cody died, he left twenty-five thousand dollars to his protégé, Jay Gatsby. However, Kaye used a legal device that Gatsby never understood to rob him of the money along with the other millions that had belonged to Cody. Ella Kaye thus inadvertently pushed Gatsby into the state of poverty that provoked him to first join the army and later to become partners with Wolfsheim.

Ewing Klipspringer

Known as "the boarder," Ewing Klipspringer always attends Gatsby's parties; he therefore epitomizes the hundreds of others who take advantage of Gatsby's generosity and who fail to demonstrate any lasting affection after Gatsby's death. Although he is mentioned in passing in the first chapter, there is a clearer vision of him later when Gatsby, Carraway, and Daisy tour Gatsby's mansion. He reluctantly plays piano at Gatsby's insistence and his presence in the mansion depends on Gatsby's goodwill toward him. After Gatsby's death, Klipspringer calls Gatsby's house and asks Carraway to mail him his tennis shoes, which he had accidentally left behind. When Carraway asks him if he will be attending the funeral, Klipspringer says he will try to attend but makes the sad excuse of having to attend a picnic.

Lucille, Her Friend, and the Three "Mr. Mumbles"

Lucille and her unnamed friend are acquaintances of Jordan Baker and speak with her and Carraway at the first of Gatsby's Saturday soirees. Her three unnamed male suitors were called the Mr. Mumbles by Carraway because they only spoke amongst themselves and not to Carraway at all. Lucille conveys the rumors initially surrounding Gatsby and the sources of his wealth.

Mr. and Mrs. McKee

Mr. and Mrs. McKee are friends of Myrtle Wilson and her sister, Catherine. They appear only at the party at the New York apartment. Mrs. McKee fawns on Myrtle, commenting first on the beauty of her dress and then on her beautiful face. The pair are present to contrast their relatively luxurious life to Myrtle's squalid life with George Wilson in Queens. Mrs. McKee also emphasizes Myrtle's mistake in marrying George with her story of almost marrying someone she later believed to be beneath her.

Michaelis

Michaelis, the young Greek man who owns a coffee shop next to George Wilson's garage, is the principal witness to the last fight between George and his wife, Myrtle, after George discovers that Myrtle is having an affair. He also witnesses George's mourning during the night following Myrtle's death. During this evening, Michaelis encourages George to go to a church to seek comfort—a suggestion George ignores. Consequently, Michaelis is uncomfortable when George tells him that he associates the sign of T. J. Eckleburg with the watchful eyes of God. Michaelis stays with George until breakfast, when he can leave the distraught man with others and catch some sleep. Later, when he returns hurriedly to the garage after four hours of sleep, George has already departed on the mission that would end in Gatsby's murder. Thus, Michaelis is the one to relate to the newspapers the events that led to the slaying of Jay Gatsby.

"Owl-eyes"

Owl-eyes appears at the beginning and the end of the novel, and he is one of the few people to be sympathetic to Gatsby's efforts at authenticity. Owl-eyes, who earns his nickname because of the heavy glasses he wears, first appears in the library as Carraway and Jordan Baker tour Gatsby's mansion. He is drunk and very impressed that the books are real; he even takes the time to show Carraway and Baker the pages in the books to verify his claim.

Owl-eyes is also one of the few people—aside from Carraway, Gatsby's father, the postman, and a few servants—to attend the funeral services. After Gatsby is buried, Owl-eyes apologizes to Carraway for not making it to the house before the ceremony. Carraway mentions that no one else did either. Owl-eyes is exasperated: "'Go on!' He started. 'Why, my God! they used to go there by the hundreds.' He took off his glasses and wiped then again, outside and in. 'The poor son-of-a-bitch,' he said."[61]

Sloane and His Lady

Sloane and his lady make a brief appearance with Tom Buchanan when the three arrive unexpectedly at Gatsby's mansion while Nick Carraway is visiting. After a terse conversation, they announce that they must depart, but Gatsby invites them to stay for dinner. The unnamed lady counters with an offer for Carraway and Gatsby to join her and Sloane for a dinner party she is giving that evening. Carraway perceives this offer to be insincere because Sloane refuses to speak directly to Gatsby. As a consequence, Carraway declines the offer, but the unwitting Gatsby accepts and excuses himself momentarily to retrieve his coat. Sloane questions Carraway on why Gatsby cannot perceive that he is really not wanted. The two, in the company of Tom Buchanan, then give Gatsby the slip. These interactions reveal the snobbery of East Egg's inhabitants as well as Gatsby's unfamiliarity with the subtleties of the wealthy elites across the bay.

George B. Wilson

George B. Wilson is the husband of Myrtle, Tom Buchanan's secret lover. Wilson owns a generally unsuccessful gas station and garage in Queens just under the bespectacled sign of Dr. T. J. Eckleburg. Wilson's initial relationship with Buchanan is that of a prospective buyer for a car he wants to fix up and sell for a profit. However, on discovering a dog leash wrapped in tissue paper on Myrtle's dresser, he learns that his wife is involved with another man. He responds by locking her in the bedroom. As a result of the discovery, Wilson makes the decision to move west, taking his wife with him.

However, when Myrtle is killed, the desperate and deranged Wilson seeks out the driver of the yellow death car, whom as he believes to be the lover of his now deceased wife. Erroneously, he connects the car with Gatsby and learns the location of Gatsby's mansion from Tom Buchanan. He murders Gatsby while he is in his pool and then commits suicide. Wilson therefore symbolizes the plight of the poor when manipulated by the wealthy. Even in his death, he unsuspectingly acts out the wishes of Buchanan, who told him how to find Gatsby.

Myrtle Wilson

Myrtle Wilson is Tom Buchanan's mistress and the wife of George Wilson, the owner of the garage and gas station in Queens. While in New York in the company of Tom and Nick Carraway, she unconvincingly acts out the role of a wealthy lady in order to feel worthy of Tom: her absolute need for a mutt off of the street—which is comically called an Airedale—and her statement that her frilly and obviously costly dress meant nothing to her. Yet these overtures are rebuffed by Tom when she later chants Daisy's name. As Parr explains,

> Myrtle . . . is ultimately the victim of illusions. Although she believes that she and Tom will marry, he clearly has no such intention. Indeed, Tom makes clear that Myrtle's place in his life is tangential when they have a

violent fight over whether or not she should be allowed to say Daisy's name. When she insists on doing so, Tom breaks her nose.[62]

When George learns of her affair, he locks her in the upstairs room, from where she watches Jordan Baker, Carraway, and Tom in Gatsby's yellow car. Carraway surmises that she mistakes Baker for Daisy. It is this error that causes her to run into the highway to chase down the returning yellow car—now being driven by Daisy with Gatsby next to her—which is the cause of her death and George's lethal search for Gatsby.

Myrtle Wilson is locked in a room by her husband after he learns of her affair with Tom.

Meyer Wolfsheim

Meyer Wolfsheim, known as the man who fixed the 1919 World Series, is Gatsby's partner in an apparent number of criminal business ventures. When Gatsby returned penniless from the war, it was Wolfsheim who discovered him. As he tells Carraway, "'I raised him out of nothing, right out of the gutter. I saw right away he was a fine-appearing, gentlemanly young man, and when he told me he was from Oggsford [Oxford] I knew I could use him good.'"[63] Wolfsheim and Gatsby subsequently formed a partnership that would be the foundation of Gatsby's incredible wealth.

Despite Wolfsheim's friendship with Gatsby, Carraway views him as a suspicious, and even villainous, character. Carraway's initial impressions at lunch, which include cufflinks made of human teeth, make him wary of Wolfsheim throughout the novel. Even after Gatsby's death, Carraway is wary of the connection that Wolfsheim might offer him, meaning he might try to lure Carraway into his lifestyle much as he did Gatsby. Of further distaste to Carraway is Wolfsheim's unwillingness to attend Gatsby's funeral, a decision Wolfsheim defends by stating that he no longer gets mixed up in the affairs of the dead.

CHAPTER FIVE

Themes in *The Great Gatsby*

P revious to World War I, the common sentiment in American life was that one could achieve whatever goals he or she could envision. Yet this idealistic vision of American life, called the American dream, faded markedly after the horrors of the war. The gruesome fighting and loss of life left a strong impression on those who returned home from the war as well as on the families whose sons were killed in Europe. This was especially true of the younger generations, which included F. Scott Fitzgerald.

However, the theme of the American dream was not the only idea to consume Fitzgerald during the years that he wrote *The Great Gatsby*. Indeed, hundreds, if not thousands, of critical studies have been written on the subject of Fitzgerald's best-known work. Of these, several major points have continued to dominate the field, including the aptness of Carraway as a narrator as well as his loss of innocence in the course of the novel, Gatsby's role not just as a lover or a criminal but also as a heroic figure, and the significance of the faded advertisement for the optometrist, Dr. T. J. Eckleburg. As each of these investigations reveals a new theme, the reader may come to a greater appreciation of the complexity and versatility of Fitzgerald's masterwork.

Gatsby's Self-Invention

The post–World War I American reality was one of loss, for the youth especially. Within the American psyche there was a profound sense that life was meaningless and that the pursuit of

The tragedies of World War I brought a sense of meaninglessness to the youth of America.

money for its own sake ignored the cultural roots—a working together for a common good—initially inspired by the American dream. Fitzgerald used this idea of rootlessness in the creation of Gatsby: Dissatisfied with his own past, Gatsby acts out for those around him the character he wishes himself to be.

Gatsby's self-invention permeates the novel. The reader learns from Carraway that James Gatz had already invented the name *Jay Gatsby* before boarding Dan Cody's yacht. Through Gatsby's confessions to Carraway, the reader learns that Gatsby misled Daisy five years earlier into thinking that he was wealthier than he was and that he used his army uniform to disguise the fact that he could not afford nicer clothes. Similarly, Gatsby disguises the source of his wealth by never confessing the illegal nature of his income to Carraway: bootlegging and selling stolen or forged bonds. In fact, Carraway does not learn of the true source of Gatsby's income until after Gatsby's death.

Indeed, it is not until just before the funeral that the reader glimpses the depth to which Gatsby's ruse ran when Henry C.

Gatz proudly displays an old copy of *Hopalong Cassidy*. On the fly-leaf of the book is a schedule Gatsby penned when he was a boy:

Rise from bed . . .	6:00	AM
Dumbbell exercise and wall-scaling . . .	6:15–6:30 ''	
Study electricity, etc. . . .	7:15–8:15 ''	
Work . . .	8:30–4:30 PM	
Baseball and sports . . .	4:30–5:00 ''	
Practice elocution, poise and how to attain it . . .	5:00–6:00 ''	
Study needed inventions . . .	7:00–9:00 ''[64]	

Gatsby's schedule shows that, even as a child, he sought to transform and improve himself.

Gatsby, in his constant need to prove himself as someone he was not, invested heavily in the expensive things with which he surrounded himself. These were the material displays for which Gatsby became known on Long Island Sound, such as his lavish parties, his mansion estate, and the yellow car that Tom Buchanan considers clownish. Yet, in the end, none of these displays of wealth were able to provide Gatsby with a sense of meaning because his love for Daisy goes unfulfilled.

The only unpurchased reality that Gatsby possessed was his love for Daisy before he went off to the war when he was still poor. It

Though Gatsby lavishly displays his wealth, he is unable to obtain the love he seeks from Daisy.

was precisely his poor financial position, however, that did not allow him the fruits of that love. Gatsby therefore sought to re-create the past by marrying Daisy, but with his new, wealthy persona intact. As critic Roger Lewis elaborates,

> When one's sense of self is self-created, when one is present at one's own creation, so to speak, one is in a paradoxical position. One knows everything about oneself that can be known, and yet the significance of such knowledge is unclear, for no outside contexts exist to create meaning. The result is that the self-created man turns to the past, for he can know that. It is an inescapable context. For Gatsby, and for the novel, the past is crucial. [65]

Like-Minded Ideals: Love and Money

However, there is more to Gatsby's pursuit of Daisy than simply an adoration of the past: He is very aware of the connection between his pursuit of money and that of Daisy. Fitzgerald makes Gatsby's adoration of Daisy the heart of the novel's plot. And Gatsby in turn becomes the only character to see clearly the connection between his quest for the ideal of love and that of wealth.

Nowhere is this more true than in the comments he makes about Daisy's voice to Carraway. As Carraway narrates,

> "She's got an indiscreet voice," I remarked. "It's full of—" I hesitated.

> "Her voice is full of money," he [Gatsby] said suddenly.

> That was it. I'd never understood before. It was full of money—that was the inexhaustible charm that rose and fell in it, the jingle of it, the cymbals' song of it. . . . High in a white palace the king's daughter, the golden girl. [66]

Carraway is taken with this comment because of the truth that rings beneath it; the charming allure of Daisy Buchanan is allied with the attraction of wealth.

What is so striking about this comment, however, is not just the insightfulness of the observation but that Gatsby is able to recognize this pursuit in himself; his capacity to love Daisy Buchanan exists because he sees the connection between love and money. Lewis states,

It is true that from Wolfsheim to Nick Carraway, people are in the East to earn their livings. . . . But Gatsby, with his boundless capacity for love, a capacity unique in the sterile world he inhabits, sees that the pursuit of money is a substitute for love. He knows himself well enough to see that his own attraction toward wealth is tied to his love for Daisy. The fact that Gatsby's money, like his love, should be self-made gives his description of her voice authority and depth.[67]

The appeal of Gatsby's romantic notions toward Daisy is the same as the appeal of wealth. Unlike Tom Buchanan, for whom wealth is simply a fact of life, Gatsby's riches are the product of a poor boy's vision. The same applies to his pursuit of Daisy: She is an ideal that he has kept with him for five years. Gatsby's accumulation of wealth is the means by which he seeks to live out his romantic fantasy.

An Ambivalent Narrator

The narrator of Gatsby's story, Nick Carraway, on the other hand, is a far more practical character and, as such, is suitable to tell the novel's story. However, the character of Carraway is marked by a need for order, which, although allowing for the story to be narrated, means that he, for the majority of the novel at least, exists in a state of relative ambivalence.

Throughout most of the novel, Carraway prides himself on his honesty. As he explains, "Everyone suspects himself of at least one of the cardinal virtues, and this is mine: I am one of the few honest people I have ever known."[68] Indeed, it is because of Carraway's self-professed honesty that he is able to narrate convincingly the adventures and misadventures of *The Great Gatsby* as the reader is able to believe and identify with him; it is his honest tolerance that makes him the ideal narrator.

Of further consequence to Carraway's ability to narrate Gatsby's story is his relative social position to the other characters of the novels. As critic A. E. Dyson explains, "Carraway is the one middle-class character in the novel—vaguely at home in the worlds both of Daisy and of Myrtle, but belonging to neither, and so able to see and judge both very clearly." Mostly due to these middle-class, Midwestern beginnings, Carraway initially seeks to reserve judgment. In explaining this, he cites the advice his father gave him when he was young: to reserve judgment of others as all the people in the world were not necessarily raised with the same social advantages that he was. Dyson further states that Carraway, "is conscious of 'advantages' of moral education that enable him to see through false romanticisms to their underlying insincerity, and savor their bitter ironies."[69]

Carraway's adherence to these principles, however, also means that he is slow to judge the events that unfold around him. David Parker, a literary critic, describes how this affects the narration:

> As he tells us himself, Nick is slow-thinking. He does not learn immediately from his experiences with Gatsby, but slowly, reluctantly, and in retrospect. At the beginning of the novel, he tells us, "When I came back from the East last autumn [after Gatsby's death] I felt that I wanted the world to be in uniform and at a sort of moral attention forever; I wanted no more riotous excursions with privileged glimpses into the human heart." Nick's slowness in learning gives an added touch of plausibility to his narration, and makes it much more dramatic for the reader, who sees him, in the course of the novel, gradually coming to a realization of what his experiences may teach him. This initial response he describes betrays the very deficiency in his character he [later] learns to correct: Nick wants the world and the people in it to be cleaner and simpler than they are.[70]

Myrtle Wilson lashes out at Tom Buchanan just before he breaks her nose.

Initially, this means that Carraway is given to a certain cold-hearted approach to the events in the novel. For example, there is a certain cold acceptance in Carraway when Tom Buchanan breaks Myrtle Wilson's nose. As Carraway relates,

> Making a short deft movement, Tom Buchanan broke her nose with his open hand.
>
> Then there were the bloody towels upon the bathroom floor, and women's voices scolding, and high over the confusion a long broken wail of pain. Mr. McKee awoke from his doze and started toward the door. . . . Taking my hat from the chandelier, I followed. [71]

Admittedly, Carraway leaves the New York apartment, but more out of a need to control his own embarrassment and drunkenness than out of any real feelings for either Myrtle or Tom. This need for control—for the world to be cleaner and simpler than it is—when combined with his self-professed need to reserve judgment, leads Carraway to be rather unattached and ambivalent for most of the novel.

Gatsby as a Heroic Romantic

Unlike the ambivalent Nick Carraway, however, F. Scott Fitzgerald was more like the character of Jay Gatsby since he was given to romanticism. In fact, Gatsby's quest for Daisy has similarities to Fitzgerald's own youthful first love. At age nineteen, Fitzgerald fell in love with the sixteen-year-old Ginevra King; yet even before King would call off the affair, Fitzgerald overheard in a conversation of her peers that a "poor boy" like Fitzgerald should not try to marry above his station. In *The Great Gatsby*, Fitzgerald uses this notion of station to reveal the very real pettiness of characters like the Buchanans in favor of the tragic but more heroic Gatsby.

Tom and Daisy share a false love for each other.

Like Fitzgerald, Gatsby is accused by Tom Buchanan of being out of his league during their fight over Daisy at the Plaza Hotel: "I'll be damned" says Tom to Gatsby, "if I see how you got in a mile of [Daisy] unless you brought the groceries to the back door."[72] Unfortunately for Gatsby, Tom is quicker to grasp the truth of the matter. Daisy does "belong" to Tom, although not in the way that he makes so crassly apparent. Instead, it is because Daisy is incapable of sharing in the idealized romantic sentiments expressed by Gatsby. As Dyson explains,

Tom has the nature of things on his side, and it is part of the nature of things that he and Daisy belong together. Daisy has to say to Gatsby not "I love you alone," but "I love you too." This "too" is Tom's victory, and he can follow it up by equating Gatsby's romance with his own hole-in-the-corner affair with Myrtle—calling it a "presumptuous little flirtation" and announcing that it is now at an end. After this Gatsby has no weapons left for the fight.[73]

The reality of Daisy is that she is too much like Tom—she is willing to use Gatsby like Tom uses Myrtle, but in the end she will, like Tom, retreat into the careless power of their money. According to Dyson,

> [Gatsby] has "broken up like glass against Tom's hard malice": and for this reason he can now be pitied, since Tom's attitude, though conclusively realistic, is also hard, and inhuman, and smaller than Gatsby's own. The reality turns out to be less admirable, less human than the fantasy. The events leading to Gatsby's death symbolize, very powerfully, that his downfall, though inevitable, is by no means an unambiguous triumph of moral powers. His death is brought about by Daisy, who first lets him shield her and then deserts him: by Tom, who directs the demented Wilson to the place where he is to be found; and by Wilson himself—a representative of the ash-gray men who comes to Gatsby, in his disillusionment, as a terrible embodiment of the realities which have killed his dream.[74]

The sympathy that Carraway feels for Gatsby as a result of Gatsby's adherence to his romantic vision is not misplaced. Carraway admits these sentiments to Gatsby on the morning after the argument between Tom and Gatsby when he calls the Buchanans and their ilk "a rotten crowd" and tells Gatsby that he is "worth the whole damn bunch put together."[75] Gatsby pays the price of death for his loyalty, but it is his willingness to adhere to his heroic passions that allows Carraway, and the reader, to overlook the faults of Gatsby and to have the most respect for him as a result.

Nick Carraway's Price: The Loss of Innocence

However, Carraway's ability to understand and even appreciate the complex character of Gatsby did not come easily. In addition to honesty, Carraway tells us that he values self-sufficiency and sticking to the rules. Although these are good traits, Carraway slowly learns that these qualities sometimes lead him to be cold and overly critical. In fact, Carraway's relationship with Jordan Baker allows him to learn how to come to terms with the complexity of himself and therefore Jay Gatsby.

Carraway's emphasis on the value of self-sufficiency is what first attracts him to Baker. However, it is Baker who exposes the limits of Carraway's honesty: He casually dismisses his discovery of Baker's dishonesty as a trait that a man must accept in a woman. As the novel progresses, Carraway becomes more and more enamored of Baker and imagines himself in love with her because she embodies those tendencies that he claims not to have. As Parker explains,

> It is fitting that Nick should toy with the idea of loving Jordan, whom he admires for her self-sufficiency. As Gatsby projects his romantic heroic dreams onto Daisy, so Nick projects his skeptical anti-heroic vision onto Jordan. . . . But where Daisy fails Gatsby by not measuring up to his vision, Jordan educates Nick by showing him the inadequacy of his.[76]

Carraway's dawning awareness of his own inadequacies comes only with the realization of Baker's. On the evening that Carraway and Baker, in the company of Tom Buchanan, discover that Myrtle was killed by Gatsby's car, Baker invites Carraway in for dinner. As Carraway narrates,

> Jordan put her hand on my arm.
>
> "Won't you come in, Nick?"
>
> "No thanks."

I was feeling a little sick and I wanted to be alone. But Jordan lingered for a moment more.

"It's only half-past nine," she said.

I'd be damned if I'd go in; I'd had enough of all of them for one day, and suddenly that included Jordan too.[77]

To Carraway's disgust, Baker expects a date. Carraway, profoundly disturbed by the day's events, declines and goes home.

The following afternoon, Carraway speaks with Baker on the telephone. Uncharacteristically, he cannot bring himself to confront the meaning of the previous day's events. Instead, their conversation simply peters out into silence, leaving Carraway to reflect that he could not remember who had hung up the phone but that he could not have talked to her that day if he "never talked to her again in this world."[78] Carraway sees Baker one

Nick's attraction to Jordan Baker fades because she points out his inadequacies.

more time. She rebukes him for his abrupt treatment of her; she says that she thought he prided himself on being a straightforward, honest person. However, Carraway no longer possesses that same surety.

Parker explains the significance of this event for Carraway:

> Nick has in fact discovered human complexity within himself. . . . Nick's rupture with Jordan shows him that honesty is not a simple value, that cleanness and simplicity are not enough in the conduct of personal relations. It marks, moreover, the beginning of Nick's maturity. . . . On reflection, Nick learns, not merely to assess experience honestly, but to accept the paradoxes of human conduct and personality, with sympathy, as well as understanding. He learns to look at life through a variety of windows, from more than one point of view, and to accept the sobering wisdom that achievement brings.[79]

This change, personified by the character of Baker and marked by Carraway's complex and not wholly honest breakup with her, is ultimately what allows him to reflect on and to appreciate Gatsby as a human being by the end of the novel. Carraway no longer expresses the same level of naive reticence and no longer feels the need to draw away from what he sees as the crux of Gatsby's strength: Gatsby's belief in the romanticized future despite the weight of the past.

The Art of *The Great Gatsby*

That such a change in Carraway's character occurs is also the result of Fitzgerald's masterful ability to tell a multifold story that includes the plights of several lives during the spring and summer of 1922. Although a short novel—a mere 218 pages in its initial publication—Fitzgerald manages to capture the attention and sympathies of his readers. One of the most remarkable aspects of the stylistic achievements that mark Fitzgerald's work as a masterpiece is his use of the narrative. Fitzgerald manages, through the personality and character of Nick Carraway, to offer his readers a number of separate writing styles, all of which are bound together in the smooth and distinct voice of Carraway.

Fitzgerald's complex method of presentation begins with Carraway declaring that his version of the tale of Gatsby is, in fact, the account currently being read. Furthermore, the reader is led to believe that all of the events that will transpire in the book have already occurred. The reader is therefore given the luxury of enjoying two distinct writing styles from the very beginning—Carraway the narrator, who is allowed to reflect on the events at his leisure, and Carraway the character, who must react to each situation as it occurs.

Fitzgerald's novel endures because of his masterful use of narrative and complex method of presentation.

Because Carraway is "writing" the tale, the reader experiences many distinctly literary passages in which Carraway has the freedom to reflect on the nature of the characters. Such is the case when he provides the more general descriptions prevalent throughout the novel, including the description of the regular preparations for Gatsby's parties or the long list of attendees who happened to pass through Gatsby's mansion during that fateful summer. Another such instance is Carraway's retelling of the events that occurred between Michaelis and George Wilson the night after Myrtle's death.

However, because Carraway is a character in his own story, the reader also experiences his immediate reactions to many of the events; in other words, we experience many of Carraway's "present" memories. For example, when he makes his first trip to the Buchanans', he comments, while at the dinner table, that "among the broken fragments of the last five minutes at table I remember the candles being lit again, and I was conscious of wanting to look squarely at every one, and yet to avoid all eyes." Another example occurs later in the novel, when he reflects on the need to break off his previous relationship before he can pursue Jordan Baker: "But I am slow-thinking and full of interior rules that act as brakes on my desires, and I knew that first I had to get myself definitely out of that tangle back home." [80]

However, Carraway's versatility as a narrator is not limited to his reflections on the past events of Gatsby or on his own current reactions to the other characters, to whom he gives voice and sentiment. One such instance involves the character of Jordan Baker. As critic George Garrett explains,

> Narrative virtuosity becomes increasingly various and complex as we move deeper into the story. In Chapter 4 we are given a first-person narration, in her own words, by Jordan Baker . . . concerning Daisy and Gatsby in 1917. This is told in a credible and appropriate vernacular for Jordan Baker—as recalled, of course, by Carraway. [81]

Another similar moment in the novel is Carraway's retelling of Gatsby's own story as a poor soldier about to go to war. Carraway goes into great detail with respect to not only Gatsby's situation but also his feelings and even his dreams. According to Carraway, Gatsby's "heart was in a constant, turbulent riot. The most grotesque and fantastic conceits haunted him in his bed at night. A universe of ineffable gaudiness spun itself out in his brain while the clock ticked on the washstand and the moon soaked with wet light his tangled clothes on the floor." [82] This aspect of Carraway's narrative allows Fitzgerald to give us the sentiments of the young Gatsby himself. Garrett elaborates on this passage: "By this time, Carraway so dominates the material of the story (even his speculation and tentativeness can be taken as the authority of integrity) that he is capable of creating a language that can dramatize in rhythmic images the inward and spiritual condition of Gatsby as a young man."[83]

Indeed, this freedom of narration even permitted the voice of the now-dead Gatsby seemingly to call out to the guilt-strewn Nick Carraway:

> But, as they drew back the sheet and looked at Gatsby with unmoved eyes, his protest continued in my brain:

> "Look here, old sport, you've got to get somebody for me. You've got to try hard. I can't go through this alone."[84]

Indeed, the voice of Nick Carraway is what allowed Fitzgerald to create such a complex and thorough novel in as little space as he did. Carraway's versatility gave Fitzgerald an edge over his characters and permits readers, through Carraway, to come to know and understand the plight of Gatsby, Baker, Daisy, Tom, Myrtle, and George Wilson. It is perhaps this stylistic mark of excellence that has helped make *The Great Gatsby* the living, breathing novel that it is today.

Notes

Introduction: The Humanity of *The Great Gatsby*

1. Quoted in Harold Bloom, ed., *Modern Critical Views: F. Scott Fitzgerald*. New York: Chelsea House, 1985, pp. 24–25.

2. F. Scott Fitzgerald, *The Great Gatsby*. New York: Scribner's, 1925, p. 182.

Chapter 1: The Life of F. Scott Fitzgerald

3. Quoted in Matthew J. Bruccoli, *Some Sort of Epic Grandeur: The Life of F. Scott Fitzgerald*, San Diego: Harcourt, Brace, Jovanovich, 1981, p. 123.

4. Quoted in Bruccoli, *Some Sort of Epic Grandeur*, p. 22.

5. Quoted in Bruccoli, *Some Sort of Epic Grandeur*, p. 23.

6. Bruccoli, *Some Sort of Epic Grandeur*, pp. 38–39.

7. Quoted in Bruccoli, *Some Sort of Epic Grandeur*, p. 37.

8. Quoted in Arthur Mizener, *The Far Side of Paradise*. Cambridge, MA: Riverside, 1949, p. 23.

9. Mizener, *The Far Side of Paradise*, p. 33.

10. Quoted in Mizener, *The Far Side of Paradise*, p. 50.

11. Quoted in Bruccoli, *Some Sort of Epic Grandeur*, p. 84.

12. Quoted in Bruccoli, *Some Sort of Epic Grandeur*, p. 84.

13. Jeffrey Myers, *Scott Fitzgerald: A Biography*. New York: Harper-Collins, 1994, p. 23.

14. Quoted in Mizener, *The Far Side of Paradise*, p. 81.

15. Quoted in Bruccoli, *Some Sort of Epic Grandeur*, p. 103.

16. Mizener, *The Far Side of Paradise*, p. 125.

17. Quoted in Bruccoli, *Some Sort of Epic Grandeur*, p. 195.

18. Quoted in Henry Dan Piper, *F. Scott Fitzgerald: A Critical Portrait*. New York: Holt, Rinehart, and Winston, 1965, p. 113.

19. Quoted in Bruccoli, *Some Sort of Epic Grandeur*, p. 424.

20. Quoted in Bruccoli, *Some Sort of Epic Grandeur*, p. 488.

Chapter 2: The Jazz Age, Gangsters, and the American Dream

21. Quoted in Kenneth Eble, *F. Scott Fitzgerald*, rev. ed. Boston: Twayne, 1977, p. 101.

22. Piper, *F. Scott Fitzgerald*, p. 159.

23. Quoted in Piper, *F. Scott Fitzgerald*, p. 159.

24. Piper, *F. Scott Fitzgerald*, p. 159.

25. Quoted in Piper, *F. Scott Fitzgerald*, p. 159.

26. Quoted in Mizener, *The Far Side of Paradise*, p. 169.

27. Quoted in Mizener, *The Far Side of Paradise*, p. 169.

28. Eble, *F. Scott Fitzgerald*, p. 101.

29. Quoted in Eble, *F. Scott Fitzgerald*, p. 101.

30. Piper, *F. Scott Fitzgerald*, p. 103.

31. Piper, *F. Scott Fitzgerald*, p. 102.

32. Fitzgerald, *The Great Gatsby*, p. 106.

33. Quoted in Piper, *F. Scott Fitzgerald*, p. 115.

34. Piper, *F. Scott Fitzgerald*, p. 114.

35. Fitzgerald, *The Great Gatsby*, p. 19.

36. Quoted in Katie de Koster, ed., *Readings on "The Great Gatsby."* San Diego: Greenhaven, 1998, pp. 41–42.

37. Quoted in de Koster, *Readings on "The Great Gatsby,"* p. 43.

38. Piper, *F. Scott Fitzgerald*, p. 114.

39. Piper, *F. Scott Fitzgerald*, p. 115.

40. Piper, *F. Scott Fitzgerald*, p. 116.

41. Quoted in Piper, *F. Scott Fitzgerald*, p. 118.

42. Fitzgerald, *The Great Gatsby*, p. 74.

43. Quoted in de Koster, *Readings on "The Great Gatsby,"* p. 45.

44. Fitzgerald, *The Great Gatsby*, p. 70.

45. Piper, *F. Scott Fitzgerald*, p. 120.

46. Fitzgerald, *The Great Gatsby*, p. 112.

47. Quoted in Bloom, *Modern Critical Views*, p. 32.

Chapter 3: Wealth, Love, and Tragedy

48. Fitzgerald, *The Great Gatsby*, p. 23.

Chapter 4: The Characters of *The Great Gatsby*

49. Quoted in Matthew Bruccoli, ed., *New Essays on "The Great Gatsby."* Cambridge, England: Cambridge University Press, 1985, p. 70.

50. Fitzgerald, *The Great Gatsby*, p. 179.

51. Quoted in A. Robert Lee, ed., *Scott Fitzgerald: The Promises of Life*. London: Vision, 1989, p. 151.

52. Fitzgerald, *The Great Gatsby*, p. 133.

53. Fitzgerald, *The Great Gatsby*, p. 134.

54. Fitzgerald, *The Great Gatsby*, pp. 180–81.

55. Fitzgerald, *The Great Gatsby*, p. 60.

56. Quoted in Bruccoli, *New Essays on "The Great Gatsby,"* p. 61.

57. Fitzgerald, *The Great Gatsby*, p. 154.

58. Quoted in Bruccoli, *New Essays on "The Great Gatsby,"* p. 63.

59. Fitzgerald, *The Great Gatsby*, p. 111.

60. Fitzgerald, *The Great Gatsby*, p. 175.

61. Fitzgerald, *The Great Gatsby*, p. 176.

62. Quoted in Bruccoli, *New Essays on "The Great Gatsby,"* p. 69.

63. Fitzgerald, *The Great Gatsby*, p. 172.

Chapter 5: Themes in *The Great Gatsby*

64. Fitzgerald, *The Great Gatsby*, p. 174.

65. Quoted in Bruccoli, *New Essays on "The Great Gatsby,"* p. 47.

66 Fitzgerald, *The Great Gatsby*, p. 120.

67. Quoted in Bruccoli, *New Essays on "The Great Gatsby,"* p. 50.

68. Fitzgerald, *The Great Gatsby*, p. 59.

69. Quoted in Arthur Mizener, ed., *F. Scott Fitzgerald: A Collection of Critical Essays*. Englewood Cliffs, NJ: Prentice-Hall, 1963, p. 115.

70. Quoted in Bloom, *Modern Critical Views*, p. 147.

71. Fitzgerald, *The Great Gatsby*, pp. 37–38.

72. Fitzgerald, *The Great Gatsby*, p. 132.

73. Quoted in Mizener, *F. Scott Fitzgerald*, p. 121.

74. Quoted in Mizener, *F. Scott Fitzgerald*, p. 122.

75. Fitzgerald, *The Great Gatsby*, p. 154.

76. Quoted in Bloom, *Modern Critical Views*, p. 150.

77. Fitzgerald, *The Great Gatsby*, p. 143.

78. Fitzgerald, *The Great Gatsby*, p. 156.

79. Quoted in Bloom, *Modern Critical Views,* pp. 150–51.

80. Fitzgerald, *The Great Gatsby,* pp. 16, 59.

81. Quoted in Bruccoli, *New Essays on "The Great Gatsby,"* p. 112.

82. Fitzgerald, *The Great Gatsby,* pp. 99–100.

83. Quoted in Bruccoli, *New Essays on "The Great Gatsby,"* p. 113.

84. Fitzgerald, *The Great Gatsby,* p. 166.

For Further Exploration

Below are some suggestions for potential essays on *The Great Gatsby*.

1. F. Scott Fitzgerald and his contemporaries are often referred to as "the lost generation" because many of them lost faith in the American way of life after World War I. Likewise, Nick Carraway also seems to lose faith in the lifestyles depicted within *The Great Gatsby*. Find examples of Carraway's criticisms of American life during the 1920s. How do these criticisms relate to the general loss of faith during the 1920s? *See* Ronald Berman, *"The Great Gatsby" and Modern Times;* Katie de Koster, ed., *Readings on "The Great Gatsby."*

2. After the death of Myrtle Wilson, her husband, George, confesses to his neighbor Michaelis that he associates the bespectacled eyes of Dr. T. J. Eckleburg with the eyes of God. However, George rejects Michaelis's suggestion that he go to church. Given the reality of the 1920s in the United States, what is Fitzgerald trying to say about the role of God in society, and why? *See* Arthur Mizener, ed., *F. Scott Fitzgerald: A Collection of Critical Essays;* Ronald Berman, *"The Great Gatsby" and Modern Times.*

3. When Daisy Buchanan, Jay Gatsby, and Nick Carraway tour Gatsby's mansion together in Chapter 5, Gatsby showers his bed with shirts in a display of wealth, and Daisy somewhat absurdly breaks into tears as a result. In fact, wealth plays a role throughout Gatsby's failed courtship of Daisy, and he even describes her voice as sounding of money. What examples show the connection between Gatsby's pursuit of Daisy and the concept of wealth? What is the meaning of this connection? *See* Ronald Berman, *"The Great Gatsby" and Modern Times.*

4. In the opening chapter Carraway, upon his return from his first evening at the Buchanans', sees Jay Gatsby for the first time. Gatsby is standing on his lawn with his arms held out toward a green light on the other side of the bay. Carraway later learns that the green light is at the end of the dock of the Buchanans' residence. Is this the light's only significance? Analyze the symbol of the green light. What does it represent for Gatsby and his motivations throughout the novel? Point to specific examples from the text and explain how they prove the claim. *See* Katie de Koster, ed., *Readings on "The Great Gatsby."*

5. In *The Great Gatsby,* Gatsby is striving to attain his dream of marrying Daisy, who he had met five years previous. Similarly, Myrtle

Wilson is trying to marry her vision of a perfect mate in her affair with Tom Buchanan. What other similarities can you find between Gatsby's situation and Myrtle's? What conclusions can be drawn? *See* Katie de Koster, ed., *Readings on "The Great Gatsby."*

6. Fitzgerald is known to have incorporated autobiographical information into his fiction, including modeling many of his characters on his wife, Zelda Sayre. In what ways do the women in *The Great Gatsby* appear to be like Zelda? What effect does this have on the novel as a whole? *See* Jeffrey Myers, *Scott Fitzgerald: A Biography.*

7. In *The Great Gatsby*, Nick Carraway accuses wealthy elites like the Buchanans and Jordan Baker of a general carelessness. What does Carraway mean when he says this? Locate examples within the novel and explain how they support the definition. *See* Ronald Berman, *"The Great Gatsby" and Modern Times.*

8. Within the novel, the reader is asked to rely on the accuracy of Nick Carraway's narrative. Thus, the reader is asked to have faith in Carraway's own declaration of honesty. Is Nick Carraway an honest and trustworthy narrator? Cite examples from the novel and explain how they support this position. *See* Katie de Koster, ed., *Readings on "The Great Gatsby."*

9. The 1920s were known as the Jazz Age or the flapper era and were, on the whole, an era of unprecedented wealth and partying amongst the younger generation. How are the parties described in *The Great Gatsby* typical of that era and what reason(s) did Fitzgerald have for making them so much a part of the novel? *See* Ronald Berman, *"The Great Gatsby" and Modern Times.*

10. Although Jay Gatsby would seem to be mostly a victim of unfortunate circumstance when he is mistakenly murdered by George Wilson, there are numerous allusions to Gatsby's involvement in criminal activities. Find these examples and use them to discuss whether Gatsby ultimately deserves his ghastly fate at the end of the novel. *See* Katie de Koster, ed., *Readings on "The Great Gatsby."*

Appendix of Criticism

Fitzgerald Reflects on the Jazz Age Generation

We were born to power and intense nationalism. We did not have to stand up in a movie house and recite a child's pledge to the flag to be aware of it. We were told, individually, and as a unit, that we were a race that could potentially lick ten others of any genus. This is not a nostalgic article for it has a point to make—but we began life in post-Fauntleroy suits (often a sailor's uniform as a taunt to Spain). Jingo was the lingo— we saw plays named *Paul Revere* and *Secret Service* and raced toy boats called the *Columbia* and the *Reliance* after the cup defenders. We carved our own swords whistling, *Way Down in Colon Town,* where we would presently engage in battle with lesser breeds. . . . That America passed away somewhere between 1910 and 1920.

F. Scott Fitzgerald,
"My Generation," *Esquire,* October 1968.

As Chronicler of the Rich

The world where a penny saved is a penny earned is the world of anti-art. The lower middle class in particular, Fitzgerald felt, were the enemies of style. He wanted a class that knows how to *use* writers, or at least desires a kind of life in which the imagination would have a chance to live. It was a hopeless dream, and in the end Fitzgerald learned two things: first, that the rich, whatever the quality of their living, regard the artist not as an ally but as a somewhat amusing *arriviste* [a visitor]; and, second, that to live the life of high style is to remain a moral child, who destroys whatever does not suit his whim. To be "rich," in the sense he dreamed, is to refuse responsibility, to deny fate, to try . . . to bribe God. There is implicit in such a life a doom as absolute as its splendor, and in this sense alone the career of the very rich is like that of the artist.

It is a vision atrocious and beautiful enough to be true, and it survives in Fitzgerald's work, despite the incoherence and sentimentality, with the force of truth. It is fitting that our chronicler of the rich be our prophet of failure. To those who plead that Fitzgerald could not live up to life and success, it can be said that at least he kept faith with death and defeat.

Leslie Fiedler, "Some Notes on
F. Scott Fitzgerald," in *F. Scott Fitzgerald:
A Collection of Critical Essays,* ed. Arthur Mizener.
Englewood Cliffs, NJ: Prentice-Hall, 1963.

A *New York Times Review* of *The Great Gatsby*

Of the many new writers that sprang into notice with the advent of the post-war period [World War I], Scott Fitzgerald has remained the steadiest performer and the most entertaining. Short stories, novels and a play have followed with consistent regularity since he became the philosopher of the flapper with *This Side of Paradise*. With shrewd observation and humor he reflected the Jazz Age. Now he has said farewell to his flappers—perhaps because they have grown up—and is writing of the other sisters that married. But marriage has not changed their world, only the locale of their parties. . . . His hurt romantics are still seeking that other side of paradise. And it might almost be said that *The Great Gatsby* is the last stage of illusion in this absurd chase. For middle age is creeping up on Mr. Fitzgerald's flappers. . . .

With sensitive insight and keen psychological observation, Fitzgerald discloses in these people a meanness of spirit, carelessness and absence of loyalties. He cannot hate them, for they are dumb in their insensate [foolish] selfishness, and only to be pitied. The philosopher of the flapper has escaped the mordant, but he has turned grave. A curious book, a mystical glamorous story of today. It takes a deeper cut at life than hitherto has been essayed by Mr. Fitzgerald. He writes well—he always has—for he writes naturally, and his sense of form is becoming perfected.

Edwin Clark, "A Farewell to Flappers,"
New York Times Review of Books, April 19, 1925.

Tragedy and Morality

The most tragic novel about life as it may be lived in and near this city [New York] seems to be F. Scott Fitzgerald's *The Great Gatsby* (Scribner), and the first story in his new collection, *All the Sad Young Men* (Scribner), seems a preliminary study for it. I do not know if Mr. Fitzgerald wrote with a moral intention, but he certainly produces a moral effect. "Monstrous dinosaurs carried these people in their mouths," you meditate, "and now look at the darned things," and being launched upon meditation, come to the depressing truth that they are what they are not in spite of money and power, but because of these.

May Lamberton Becker, *Saturday
Review of Literature*, June 12, 1926.

Daisy and 1920s Riches

What seems to attract [Jay Gatsby] to Daisy is the sense of financial security that she emanates: she has always been, and somehow always will be, abundantly, aboundingly rich. She is the tinselly department store window at Christmastime to the urchin in the street. Her very voice, as Gatsby puts it, "is full of money."

Fitzgerald is a courageous author. For what is Daisy, dreadful Daisy, but his dream and the American dream at that? He seems to make no bones about it. Vapid, vain, heartless, self-absorbed, she is still able to dispel a charm the effect of which on Gatsby is simply to transform him into

95

a romantic hero. The American dream, then, is an illusion? Certainly. It is all gush and twinkle. But nonetheless its effect on a sentient observer is about all life has to offer.

Is Fitzgerald then seriously telling us that to fall in love with a beautiful heiress with a monied laugh, even if she's superficial, selfish and gutless, is a fitting goal for a man's life, and one to justify years of criminal activity? Perhaps not quite. What he may be telling us is that he, the author, by creating the illusion of that illusion, may be doing the only thing worth doing in this vale of constant disillusionment.

> Louis Auchincloss, "The American
> Dream: All Gush and Twinkle," in *Readings
> on "The Great Gatsby,"* ed. Katie
> de Koster. San Diego: Greenhaven, 1998.

An Ambivalent Nick Carraway and Jordan Baker

Carraway's personality and its contextual value system emerge most definitely in his relationship with Jordan Baker. Insofar as sexual relationships reveal a cultural milieu, Nick's relationship parallels Gatsby's with Daisy. The difference consists in Carraway's lack of imaginative intensity and in his incapacity to integrate perspectives of class, morality, manners, and chronology, to see events and relationships going through aesthetic changes. Again ambivalence is the keynote. On the one hand Nick would like to join society, but on the other what is freedom to Jordan and to the Buchanans is irresponsible license according to the Carraway almanac.

> John F. Callahan, *The Illusions
> of a Nation: Myth and History
> in the Novels of F. Scott Fitzgerald*. Urbana:
> University of Illinois Press, 1972.

Car Imagery

Gatsby's car is an adolescent's dream, the very vehicle for one who formed his values as a teenager and never questioned them again. Gatsby is not sufficiently creative to choose a truly unique machine, so he selects a copy of the gaudy dream car spun from the lowest common denominator of intelligence and imagination. Such a car is exactly what an artist might fashion if he were third-rate specifically because he had plagiarized from the common American dream; because he has seen no reason for originality; because he has failed to distinguish between romance and reality. Just as Gatsby—part the shadowy gangster who made millions, part the man who could remain faithful to an ideal love for five years—is an odd mixture of pragmatist and romantic, so his car blends colors representing both traits. It is a rich cream color, a combination of the white of the dream and the yellow of money, of reality in a narrow sense. After Myrtle Wilson's death, a witness to the accident describes the car as just yellow, which, as color imagery unfolds, becomes purely and simply corruption. White, the color of his dream, has been removed from the mixture. Only the corruption, the foul dust, remains of Gatsby's dream after that hot day in New York. Thus the car becomes one external symbol of Gatsby, his mind, and what happens to his dream.

Dan Seiters, Image Patterns in the
Novels of F. Scott Fitzgerald.
Ann Arbor, MI: UMI Research, 1986.

The Heroines of *The Great Gatsby*

[In *The Great Gatsby*,] the role of heroine is split . . . among three women, each of whom is, as it were, assigned to one man. Of course heroine is the wrong term, but we should not discount the extent to which the characters reflect and reflect on each other. Jordan Baker, first presented as indistinguishable from Daisy ("two young women . . . in white") turns out to represent a sort of masculine aspect or alternative: she has, along with her name and (sporting) activity, taken on the masculine function of lying about the woman, that is herself. And Myrtle, Tom's vulgar mistress who is presumable beneath illusion or even the right to speak Daisy's name (she is slugged for doing so), nevertheless reveals the twin-ship in her own flower name, not to mention her sharing of Daisy's husband; she is a heroine in the *poetical role* which she, like Gatsby, finally plays: she dies, and in death achieves the dignity at least of surrendering her "tremendous vitality." But her closest link to Gatsby, and the most important if least remarked clue to the centrality of doubles in fiction, lies in her other name. Myrtle "returns" from the dead in the person of her avenging husband, who murders the hero and then himself.

Elizabeth Kaspar Aldrich, "'The Most Poetical
Topic in the World': Women in the Novels of
F. Scott Fitzgerald," in Scott Fitzgerald:
The Promises of Life, ed. A. Robert Lee.
London: Vision, 1989.

The Eyes of Eckleburg

The cause of the horror is, in *The Great Gatsby*, the terrifying contrast between the Buchanans, Jordan Baker, the obscene barflies who descend in formless swarms on Gatsby's house, all symbolized by the gritty, disorganized ash heaps with their crumbling men, and the solid ordered structure so paradoxically built upon sand (or ashes) which Gatsby's great dream lends to his life. And over it all brood the eyes of Dr. Eckleburg, symbols— of what? Of the eyes of God, as Wilson, whose own world disintegrates with the death of Myrtle, calls them? As a symbol of Gatsby's dream, which like the eyes is pretty shabby after all and scarcely founded on the "hard rocks" Carraway admires? Or . . . do not the eyes, in spite of everything they survey, perhaps even because of it, serve both as a focus and an unde-viating base, a single point of reference in the midst of a monstrous disor-der?

Tom Burnham, "The Eyes of Dr. Eckleburg: A Re-Examination of *The Great Gatsby*," in *F. Scott Fitzgerald: A Collection of Critical Essays*, ed. Arthur Mizener, Englewood Cliffs, NJ: Prentice-Hall, 1963.

Scott Fitzgerald, Author, Dies at Age Forty-Four

Mr. Fitzgerald in his life and writings epitomized "all the sad young men" of the post-war generation. With the skill of a reporter and the ability of an artist he captured the essence of a period when flappers and gin and "the beautiful and the damned" were the symbols at the carefree madness of an age.

Roughly, his own career began and ended with the Nineteen Twenties. *This Side of Paradise*, his first book, was published in the first year of that decade of skyscrapers and short skirts. Only six others came between it and his last, which, not without irony, he called *Taps at Reveille*. That was published in 1935. Since then a few short stories, the script of a moving picture or two, were all that came from his typewriter. The promise of his brilliant career was never fulfilled.

The best of his books, the critics said, was *The Great Gatsby*. When it was published in 1925 this ironic tale of life on Long Island at a time when gin was the national drink and sex the national obsession (according to the exponents of Mr. Fitzgerald's school of writers), it received critical acclaim. In it Mr. Fitzgerald was at his best, which was, according to John Chamberlain, his "ability to catch . . . the flavor of a period, the fragrance of a night, a snatch of an old song, in a phrase."

New York Times, "Scott Fitzgerald, Author Dies at 44," December 23, 1940.

The Influence of *The Great Gatsby*

One group of American writers who have a surprising affinity for Fitzgerald are those who seriously practice the craft of mystery writing, using the "hard-boiled detective" genre. One of the foremost of them, Raymond Chandler, was an admirer of Fitzgerald's craftsmanship. In a 1950 letter Chandler described Fitzgerald's literary distinction as "one of the rarest qualities in all literature," a kind of "charm—charm as [poet John] Keats would have used it. . . . It's not a matter of pretty writing or clear style. It's a kind of subdued magic, controlled and exquisite, the sort of thing you get from good string quartets. Yes, where would you find that today?" A few years later, drawing another analogy to romantic poetry, Chandler alluded to Fitzgerald in *The Long Goodbye:* a farewell note from a man [whom] detective Marlowe had been tracing is signed "Roger (F.

Scott Fitzgerald) Wade." The man's wife tells Marlowe that her husband had been a great admirer of Fitzgerald. . . .

Jack Kerouac, quintessential 1950's Beat Generation social rebel, would seem an unlikely disciple of Fitzgerald's work, but his 1959 picaresque work *Doctor Sax* bears this tribute:

> It was a funny song, at the end it had that 1930's lilt so hysterical Scott Fitzgerald, with writhely women squirmelying their we-a-ares in silk and brocade shiny New Year's Eve nightclub dresses with thrown champagne and popples bursting "Gluyr! the New Year's Parade!" . . .

A more widely known tribute to *The Great Gatsby* is expressed by Holden Caulfield, the urban Huckleberry Finn of J. D. Salinger's *Catcher in the Rye*. Holden himself has become one of the most enduring and endearing figures of American fiction, threading his way through the streets and neuroses of modern America, as well as through—according to a recent paperback copy—thirty hardbound and eighty-two paperback printings. A symbol of alienated youth to the young readers of the 1950's, Holden has come to be placed in a more romantic line of descent linking him to Mark Twain's Huck. That Jay Gatsby is also of that lineage, in Salinger's eyes, is evidenced by Holden's comments on the literary tastes his brother is attempting to develop in him:

> I still don't see how he could like a phony book like [Hemingway's *A Farewell to Arms*] and still like that one by Ring Lardner or that other one he's so crazy about, *The Great Gatsby*. . . . I was crazy about *The Great Gatsby*. Old Gatsby. Old sport. That killed me.

That Holden was speaking for Salinger as well as for himself in his admiration for the (surprisingly) un-phony Gatsby is reinforced by Gatsby-esque qualities in *Catcher*: a theme of revolt against the corruption of American innocence and a protagonist whose dreams are shattered by reality. Salinger's admiration was further expressed in a letter to a friend: "Re-read a lot of Scott Fitzgerald's work this week. God, I love that man. Damn fool critics are forever calling writers geniuses for their idiosyncrasies—Hemingway for his reticent dialogue, [Tom] Wolfe for his gargantuan energy, and so on. Fitzgerald's only pure idiosyncrasy was his pure brilliance."

Richard Anderson, "Gatsby's Long Shadow:
Influence and Endurance," in
New Essays on "The Great Gatsby," ed.
Matthew Bruccoli. Cambridge, England:
Cambridge University Press, 1985.

Chronology

1896
Francis Scott Key Fitzgerald is born on September 24 in Saint Paul, Minnesota.

1898–1908
His father, Edward Fitzgerald, is employed by Proctor and Gamble; family lives in Buffalo and Syracuse.

1900
Zelda Sayre is born on July 24 in Montgomery, Alabama.

1901
Fitzgerald's only surviving sibling, Annabel, is born in July while in Syracuse.

1908
Edward Fitzgerald loses his job, and the family moves back to Saint Paul; Fitzgerald attends Saint Paul Academy.

1909
Fitzgerald publishes his first story, "The Mystery of the Raymond Mortgage," in his school's journal, *Now and Then*.

1911
Fitzgerald is sent to the Newman School in Hackensack, New Jersey, because of poor academic performance at Saint Paul Academy.

1913
Enrolls at Princeton in September.

1914
The play *Fie! Fie! Fi-Fi!* is accepted by the Triangle Club; Fitzgerald meets Ginevra King in December and begins a two-year courtship.

1914–1918
World War I; the United States enters the war in 1917.

1915
Fitzgerald leaves Princeton in December because of ill health and low grades.

1916
Repeats his junior year at Princeton.

1917
Leaves Princeton without a degree in October; receives a commission as second lieutenant in the army and leaves for Fort Leavenworth on November 20; the Eighteenth Amendment to the U.S. Constitution makes alcoholic beverages illegal (it goes into effect in 1919).

1918
Fitzgerald transfers to Camp Sheridan, near Montgomery, Alabama; he completes the first draft of *The Romantic Egoist* in March; he receives news that Ginevra King is to be married; he meets eighteen-year-old Zelda Sayre that summer; World War I ends on November 11.

1919
Fitzgerald is discharged from the army on February 18; he takes a job with an advertising agency in New York; at night he writes stories, which are all rejected by publishers; he quits his job in July and returns to Saint Paul to rewrite the novel *This Side of Paradise*, which is accepted by Scribner's on September 16; from September to December, he writes and sells nine stories.

1920
This Side of Paradise is published on March 26; Fitzgerald marries Zelda Sayre on April 3 in New York; the short-story collection *Flappers and Philosophers* is published.

1921
Fitzgerald takes his first trip to Europe with pregnant Zelda on May 3; they return to the United States in July; their daughter, Frances Scott "Scottie," is born on October 26 in Saint Paul.

1922
The Beautiful and Damned is published on March 4 and *Tales of the Jazz Age* in September; in October the Fitzgeralds move to a rented house in Great Neck, New York, for twenty months after being unable to make ends meet; James Joyce publishes *Ulysses;* T. S. Eliot publishes *The Waste Land*.

1923
The Vegetable opens and closes in Atlantic City on November 19; from November to April, Fitzgerald produces eleven short stories and earns seventeen thousand dollars; Adolf Hitler writes *Mein Kampf.*

1924
The Fitzgeralds take a second trip to Europe in May and live abroad for two and a half years; Zelda begins a short-lived affair with the French aviation officer Edouard Josanne.

1925
The Great Gatsby is published on April 10; Fitzgerald meets Ernest Hemingway later that year; a third short-story collection, *All the Sad Young Men,* is also published.

1926
Fitzgerald returns to the United States in December; with his assistance, Hemingway publishes *The Sun Also Rises.*

1927
In January, Fitzgerald goes to Hollywood for his first writing assignment for the movie industry (United Artists); he moves to Delaware in March.

1928
Fitzgerald spends the summer in Paris.

1929
He begins a second two-and-a-half-year stay in Europe; William Faulkner publishes *The Sound and the Fury;* the stock market crash ushers in the Great Depression.

1929–1937
The Great Depression.

1930
In April, Zelda has the first of her breakdowns and is sent to Switzerland for treatment.

1931
Edward Fitzgerald dies in January; in September, Fitzgerald returns permanently to the United States; he begins to work for MGM in Hollywood until January 1932.

1932
Zelda experiences another breakdown and enters a clinic in Baltimore; she is diagnosed as schizophrenic and is in and out of sanitariums for the rest of Fitzgerald's life.

1933
The Eighteenth Amendment is repealed, ending Prohibition; President Franklin Roosevelt introduces the New Deal programs in an effort to end the Great Depression.

1934
Tender is the Night is published on April 12.

1935
Fitzgerald begins to write the Crack-Up stories, a collection of dark, autobiographical essays; he publishes the short-story collection *Taps at Reveille*.

1936
Fitzgerald's mother dies in September.

1936–1939
The Spanish Civil War.

1937
Fitzgerald signs a six-month contract with MGM for one thousand dollars a week which is later extended for an additional twelve months; he meets Sheilah Graham, with whom he lives until his death; Japan invades China.

1938
MGM does not renew Fitzgerald's contract; Germany invades Austria.

1939
Fitzgerald begins work on *The Last Tycoon*; he struggles as a freelance writer in Hollywood; John Steinbeck publishes *The Grapes of Wrath*.

1939–1945
World War II; the United States enters the war in 1941, after the December 7 bombing of Pearl Harbor by the Japanese.

1940
Fitzgerald continues work on his last novel, *The Last Tycoon*; he has his first heart attack on November 28; he dies from a second heart attack on December 21.

1941
The unfinished novel *The Last Tycoon* is published posthumously under the editorial direction of Edmund Wilson.

1945
The Crack-Up, composed of the Crack-Up stories, is edited by Edmund Wilson and is published.

1948
Zelda dies in a fire at Highland Sanitarium on March 10.

Works Consulted

Major Editions of *The Great Gatsby*

F. Scott Fitzgerald, *The Great Gatsby*. New York: Scribner's, 1925. The very rare first printing of F. Scott Fitzgerald's third novel.

———, *The Great Gatsby*. New York: Scribner's, 1995. This paperback edition is the most common version of *The Great Gatsby* in print.

———, *Trilmachio*. Cambridge, England: Cambridge University Press, 2000. This is the recently published first version of *The Great Gatsby* before Fitzgerald substantially altered the manuscript in galley proof form, a change that included the title.

Letters

F. Scott Fitzgerald, *The Letters of F. Scott Fitzgerald*. Ed. Andrew Turnbill. New York: Scribner's, 1963. A collection of Fitzgerald's surviving letters, including those to Zelda Sayre, Ernest Hemingway, Dorothy Parker, Sheilah Graham, and his daughter.

Biographies of F. Scott Fitzgerald

Matthew J. Bruccoli, *Some Sort of Epic Grandeur: The Life of F. Scott Fitzgerald*. San Diego: Harcourt, Brace, Jovanovich, 1981. In one of the most complete and authoritative of biographies, Bruccoli examines the life, loves, and difficulties of F. Scott Fitzgerald.

Kenneth Eble, *F. Scott Fitzgerald*. Rev. ed. Boston: Twayne, 1977. The revised addition of Eble's first Fitzgerald biography, originally published in 1963. Eble discusses how Fitzgerald's short fiction was both a product of and mirror into his life.

Sheilah Graham, *The Real F. Scott Fitzgerald: Thirty-Five Years Later*. New York: Grosset and Dunlap, 1976. A reflective and very personal look into the life, motivations, and sentiments of Fitzgerald, as written by his last great love.

Arthur Mizener, *The Far Side of Paradise*. Cambridge, MA: Riverside, 1949. A comprehensive critical biography that begins with the awareness of Fitzgerald's tendency to include even his most private of moments in his fiction.

Jeffrey Myers, *Scott Fitzgerald: A Biography*. New York: HarperCollins, 1994. In one of the newest of biographies on Fitzgerald, the author offers fresh insight about Fitzgerald, his work, and the people with whom he surrounded himself throughout his life.

Henry Dan Piper, *F. Scott Fitzgerald: A Critical Portrait*. New York: Holt, Rinehart, and Winston, 1965. A comprehensive and fluidly written critical biography of Fitzgerald and his novels. Piper takes the reader through the stages of Fitzgerald's successes and failures with an acute eye for how a writer works.

Historical Materials

Ronald Berman, *"The Great Gatsby" and Modern Times*. Urbana: University of Illinois Press, 1994. Berman looks at Fitzgerald's most famous novel in terms of the cultural context under which it was written—the 1920s. In so doing, Berman discusses how film, advertising, notions of class, and new technology affected the technique and style of Fitzgerald.

John F. Callahan, *The Illusions of a Nation: Myth and History in the Novels of F. Scott Fitzgerald*. Urbana: University of Illinois Press, 1972. Callahan explores the novels of Fitzgerald, including *The Great Gatsby*, as an overview of the struggle between property and the pursuit of wealth within American history.

Literary Criticism

Harold Bloom, ed., *Modern Critical Views: F. Scott Fitzgerald*. New York: Chelsea House, 1985. Renowned Yale professor and literary critic Harold Bloom edited this collection of critical essays, which includes some of the most influential literary thinkers of our time. Essays include: "Scott Fitzgerald and the Collapse of the American Dream," in which author Marius Bewley discusses the works of Fitzgerald by analyzing the illusory elements of the world of Jay Gatsby; Kenneth Eble's "*The Great Gatsby* and the American Novel"; and David Parker's "*The Great Gatsby*: Two Versions of the Hero," a look at the heroic, romantic role of Jay Gatsby.

Matthew Bruccoli, ed., *New Essays on "The Great Gatsby."* Cambridge, England: Cambridge University Press, 1985. This collection of essays is edited by Matthew Bruccoli, one of the most renowned and influential Fitzgerald scholars. It includes Richard Anderson's "Gatsby's Long Shadow: Influence and Endurance," in which the author looks at the influence of Fitzgerald's greatest work on literature, writers, film, and popular culture; George Garrett's "Fire and Freshness: A Matter of Style in *The Great Gatsby*," an essay that looks at the narrative art and genius of Fitzgerald's novel construction and writing style; Robert Lewis's, "Money, Love, and Aspiration in *The Great Gatsby*"; and Susan Resnesck Parr's, "The Idea of Order at West Egg," which looks at the need for order as a component of character motivations, including Nick Carraway's seeming ambivalence as a narrator.

Katie de Koster, ed., *Readings on "The Great Gatsby."* San Diego: Greenhaven, 1998. A unique and comprehensive collection of critical and historical essays that reflect a number of critical points of view with respect to *The Great Gatsby.* Essays include selections related to *The Great Gatsby* from Louis Auchincloss's *The Style's the Man: Reflections on Proust, Fitzgerald, Wharton, Vidal, and Others,* under the title "The American Dream: All Gush and Twinkle," which analyzes the reality behind the illusions in *The Great Gatsby;* William Goldhurst's "The Cynical Views of an American Literary Generation," an excerpt from *F. Scott Fitzgerald and His Contemporaries;* and Thomas H. Pauly's "Gatsby as Gangster," which demonstrates parallels between the character of Gatsby and the realities of gangsterism in the 1920s.

A. Robert Lee, ed, *Scott Fitzgerald: The Promises of Life.* London: Vision, 1989. A collection of critical essays compiled by the senior lecturer in English at the University of Kent. It includes Elizabeth Kaspar Aldrich's, "'The Most Poetical Topic in the World': Women in the Novels of F. Scott Fitzgerald," in which she examines the dual roles of Fitzgerald's female characters and attributes their various symbolic roles to Fitzgerald's mastery as a writer and Owen Dudley Edwards's "The Lost Teigueen: F. Scott Fitzgerald's Ethics and Ethnicity," which looks at the reemergence of Fitzgerald appreciation during the 1950s.

Arthur Mizener, ed., *F. Scott Fitzgerald: A Collection of Critical Essays.* Englewood Cliffs, NJ: Prentice-Hall, 1963. A very comprehensive and revealing selection of essays that discuss the career, work, and influences of F. Scott Fitzgerald. It includes Marius Bewley's "Scott Fitzgerald's Criticism of America," in which the author discusses the theme of the withering American dream within *The Great Gatsby;* Tom Burnham's "The Eyes of Dr. Eckleburg: A Re-Examination of *The Great Gatsby,*" an analysis of judgment and carelessness; "*The Great Gatsby:* Thirty-Six Years After," in which A. E. Dyson looks at Gatsby's dreams as inseparable from the human condition; Leslie Fiedler's "Some Notes on F. Scott Fitzgerald"; and the editor's own, "The Maturity of Scott Fitzgerald," which examines the sophistication of Fitzgerald's fiction and essays.

Dan Seiters, *Image Patterns in the Novels of F. Scott Fitzgerald.* Ann Arbor, MI: UMI Research, 1986. Seiters looks at the recurrent imagery in Fitzgerald's novels, giving new meaning to symbols and themes that may otherwise have gone unnoticed in both consistency and impact.

Index

Picture Credits

About the Author

Michael J. Wyly received his master of fine arts degree in creative writing from California State University, Long Beach, where he is currently an instructor of English literature and language. He has also worked as a fiction and poetry editor for several small-press publications. Wyly is currently on leave from his teaching duties and lives and writes in France.